Dear Diary:

An Elvis Fan Remembers

Copyright

Dear Diary: An Elvis Fan Remembers

Copyright © 2012 by Sandra Ann Falcetta

ISBN: 978-0-9773511-5-2

All rights reserved, including the rights to reproduce this book, portions, or photos, thereof, in any form current or future, including electronic and physical. No one may reproduce any portion, or in whole, of this work without express written consent of the author.

Printed in the United States of America

Dedication

This book is dedicated to the three most important women in my life:

Charlene Ruth Pupek

My mother and dearest friend. I was free to discuss anything with her at any time.

She loved with all her heart. I love her and always will. I will NEVER forget you, Mom!

I'll see you in Heaven soon!

Bonnie Lee Schmuck

My best friend in school and my roomie in Memphis. We were sisters in Christ which made our friendship even deeper. She's with Mom in Heaven.

See you, too, Bon!

April Raynell

She was zany, crazy, and loving. My Memphis and Hollywood buddy. Say hello to Mom and Bonnie for me!

See ya later!

Forward

In February, 1960, Elvis Presley ended his days marching for the United States Army and marched right into my heart. I was young, lonely, shy, and searching for a never ending love. I found it in the blue eyes and beautiful voice of a man in Memphis, TN. He had a rags to riches background, loved his family and country. He was my knight in shining armor.

There was never any doubt in my mind that I would meet Elvis. I just had to be patient and wait for the right time. On August 12, 1962, my dream came true. I was introduced to him personally. We shook hands and spoke for a short while. This was the beginning of a whirlwind of memories for me. I am sharing these factual events that I have treasured in my personal diaries over the years. Please enjoy as you gain a new perspective of the greatest entertainer that ever existed!

Sandy Falcetta

Table of Contents

The Beginning Years 1
 1958 1
 1959 2
 1960 3
 1961 5
 1962 11
 1963 21
 1964 24
 1966 25
 1967 25
 1968 28
 1969 29
 1970 33
 1971 35

The Memphis Years, 1972-1976 37
 1972 37
 1973 50
 1974 76
 1975 103
 1976 116

The Final Years, 1977-2012 31
 1977 31
 1978 138
 1979 142
 1980 142
 1981 143
 1982 143
 1983 143
 1984 143
 1985 145
 1986 145
 1997 146
 2000 146
 2001 147
 2005 147

2006 148
2008 148
2009 149
2010 149
2011 149
2012 150

The Future 153

The Beginning Years

1958-1971

1958

March 16, 1958   Dear Diary: today is my 10th birthday. Mom gave me this book as a gift. It has a lock and key, so I can write all my secrets in it like all my friends do in theirs. I love it! Mom and Dad invited all our family and friends over for a party for me. We ate burgers and hot dogs and had my favorite chocolate cake and ice cream and drinks. I got a lot of nice gifts—candy, money, clothes and a Revlon doll! Dad took the hi fi and records down stairs so we could dance. Most of the songs were rock n roll sung by Fats Domino, Pat Boone and a guy named Elvis Presley. I saw Elvis on TV with Ed Sullivan, Steve Allen and Milton Berle. He has long hair and he moves around and makes faces when he sings. He must be scared because his whole body shakes most of the time. All the girls cry and scream. So funny and crazy. I like his songs.

March 24, 1958   Elvis Presley left Memphis, Tenn. for training in the Army. He'll be in for two years. People are saying his singing career is over now. There are a lot of singers trying to sound like him. Some churches are burning his records. They say he's evil. Some people say he's a Communist. His mom was really crying a lot. Fans were crying, too. It doesn't make sense to me. It's the duty of all the guys to go into the service to train to protect our country. Glad I'm a girl.

APRIL 1, 1958   I have seen all of Elvis' movies several times. It doesn't cost anything. Mom gives me 25 cents for popcorn and a taffy apple. We waited in line for an hour to see "Love Me Tender." Half the movie was over before Elvis came on screen. All the girls screamed. He was plowing. His older brother, Vance, went to serve in the Civil War. They thought he was dead. Clint (Elvis) married Vance's girlfriend, Kathy. Vance came home. Lots of problems. Movie was OK. I liked the songs he sang. He died in the end. I cried. It was a western. "Loving You" was pretty close to Elvis' real life. A young guy becomes a famous singer. Lots of good songs. I liked this movie better. In "Jailhouse Rock," Elvis killed a man in a fight and went to jail. His cellmate was a country singer and taught Vince (Elvis) how to sing and play a guitar. He became a popular rock n roll singer and actor. He was injured in a fight. The doctors weren't sure his voice would be the same after he healed. In the end, he was able to sing in his beautiful voice! When he sang "You're So Young and Beautiful," I cried so hard! I loved all the songs. After seeing the movie 4 times, I knew I was in love with Elvis! In "King Creole," Elvis was a singer again. Lived in New Orleans. Good songs.

AUGUST 14, 1958   Elvis' mother, Gladys, died. She had a heart attack. News reports show him crying so hard. He must have really loved her. He had a twin brother, Jesse Garon, who died at birth. His dad has a bad back and can't work. Gladys had to work to support them. I feel sorry for Elvis. I don't want to even think about my Mom going to Heaven. I couldn't live without her.

1959

APRIL, 1959   I became a woman today. I started my period. Excited but scared. Great-Grandma Travis died. She was 100 years old. Mom and Dad went to KY for the funeral. They will be home in a few days.

JUNE 1, 1959   Sandy R. and her family have been friends with us ever since I can remember. She's a teenager and takes me to the Cotillion next door to the church every Saturday afternoon. Boys and girls go there to dance, eat snacks, and have fun. They don't know I'm not a teen yet. All the guys sit on one side of the room and the girls on the other. Sometimes a guy will ask a girl to dance, but mostly the girls dance together. So much fun! I love it! Most of the songs are rock n roll, especially Elvis.

SEPTEMBER 8, 1959   We have been attending East Gary Christian Church. I was baptized today, and I wasn't even scared! I'm afraid of drowning and I don't like my head under water. It went so fast that I didn't notice. I feel the Holy Spirit inside me. We are having a revival.

SEPTEMBER 10, 1959   Mom and Dad were baptized. Tony will wait until he's older.

OCTOBER, 1959   I wear a bra now. Mom and Dad can't believe it cuz I'm so skinny. The girls at school are jealous. The boys keep snapping my bra. I'm embarrassed. The teacher tells them to stop, but they go by my desk every chance they get. I hate it!

1960

FEBRUARY, 1960   Elvis was released from the Army. He sure is handsome! He has the most beautiful blue eyes, like mine. I read every magazine article and collect his pictures. I write him every week. I am in love with him, and I want to marry him. He has 2 girlfriends—Anita Wood in Memphis and Priscilla Beaulieu in Germany. She's only a couple years older than me, so age won't make any difference to him. I fall asleep every night crying and praying to meet him. I dream about him. I LOVE HIM SO MUCH! Elvis' dad, Vernon, married a woman named Dee. Elvis didn't go to the wedding. She is divorced and has 3 sons. Elvis has brothers now.

MAY 12, 1960   Elvis was on TV! Frank Sinatra had a welcome home party for him! I couldn't sit still in school. He is even more handsome than ever. There's a big write up in TV GUIDE. He sang "Stuck on You." He and Frank sang a couple songs together. Frank's daughter, Nancy, was on, too. I read that she has a crush on Elvis. Sammy Davis, Jr. sang also. A great show, but Elvis was the best. Now I know why girls scream when he moves. I get a funny feeling inside. I can't explain it. I guess that's the way love is. I do love him.

AUGUST, 1960   We moved a lot lately. I hate it. I make new friends, and it's time to move again. We're living with Aunt Lizzie again. I love her. She's good to us. I sleep in her room. She said I could put Elvis pictures on the walls. There's not an empty space on the walls! They're covered with Elvis! I have a life size picture from Monica. She gets a magazine from Sweden that sends a different section every month. I have his head, shoulders and outstretched arms. I wanted the whole thing, but her subscription ran out. Aunt Liz has a hi fi so I listen to Elvis records and dance. It helps me with the loneliness. Elvis' new movie, "G.I. Blues," is great! Lots of singing. He has to babysit! It's so funny! He does not know how to take care of the baby! Juliette Prowse co-starred. She's a great dancer. Rumors are she and Elvis are dating. But, Anita Wood is in Memphis waiting for him. And Priscilla Beaulieu is supposed to be his girlfriend, too. I don't understand what's going on. I just know I love him.

SEPTEMBER 1, 1960   School started today. I'm in 7th grade at Lew Wallace. It's so big. I have classes in all 3 buildings. I have to run outside after each class. No matter how cold it is, we can't take our coats with us. The grades are 7-12. I hate gym class! We have to swim! I don't know how. I wear mascara and lipstick now.

SEPTEMBER 14, 1960   I made some friends. June, Mary Kay, and twins Cathy and Carol. We have a lot of fun at lunch. We walk to the drug store and look at magazines. I told them I'm gonna marry Elvis. They tease me about it. They call me Mrs. Presley. Kids are staring at me and asking if I really am married to him. My friends tell them yes. We laugh about it.

SEPTEMBER 15, 1960   Lots of kids are asking me for my autograph. I sign MY name and they get mad. They want me to sign Mrs. Elvis Presley. I do and laugh.

SEPTEMBER 16, 1960   Kids of all ages and even teachers at school won't leave me alone! They box me in and want my autograph! I'm so scared! School security took me to the guidance counselor's office to talk. I told her it was a joke but the kids won't believe me. Someone walks me to class every day, and I have to report to the guidance counselor for lunch hour for my safety. I don't know how Elvis puts up with the mobs. The counselor has me look at stupid pictures and tell her what I see. She asks me questions about my life at home. She even called Mom and asked to see her. Mom said no and told her to leave me alone cuz I'll get over this little crush on Elvis. I cry so much. I want to move. I hate this school! I write Elvis and tell him all the problems I have.

OCTOBER, 1960   Kids don't bother me as much now. I can go to lunch with my friends. Saw "Flaming Star." It's a western. Elvis is a half-breed Indian. He dies in the end. Not too many songs. OK, but I'm not crazy about it.

DECEMBER 25, 1960   Got new clothes, stuffed animals, and Elvis records for Christmas. It was a nice day. Everyone came for dinner and to exchange gifts. I'm glad school is out. Elvis broke his pinky playing football.

1961

MAY 10, 1961   I had a bad day at school. When I got home, Mom was dancing around the kitchen singing, "You got a letter. Guess who it's from?" "Gearldine," I answered. Mom was laughing and dancing and waving the letter. I wasn't in the mood, and it made me mad. She finally held it up to my face. The return address was: Elvis Presley 3764 Highway 51 South, Memphis, Tenn. I dropped my books! I screamed and so did Mom! I was jumping all around the room. "Let me have it!" I pleaded. Mom continued to tease me and wave the letter. Finally, she opened the end with a knife and gave me the letter. I was shaking and crying. After all these months, Elvis answered me! He knows I exist! He wrote me! I thought it would be typed, but it was hand written. By Elvis! It says: "Dear Sandy: I just boarded the airplane here in Honolulu to head back to Hollywood and thought you might be interested to know what I've been up to lately. For the past month we have been filming "Blue Hawaii" over on the Hawaiian Islands. The scenery there is just gorgeous. The weather was always nice and everyone was so friendly. I really enjoyed working there. After completing the rest of the film in Hollywood, I will return home – to Memphis around the first of June. I see the stewardess serving dinner, so I'd better sign off for now. Take good care of yourself and write soon! Sincerely, Elvis Presley" I am so shocked and happy! I can't stop laughing and crying. Dad was even surprised, when he came home. He added to the excitement by saying he and Mom have been talking about building a new house in Merrillville, a suburb of Gary! We'll be moving before school starts! I'm so excited!!

MAY 11, 1961   I took my letter to school to show my friends and teachers. I went to the guidance counselor for my weekly visit. She was shocked about the letter. She said it was a copy of a letter, not the original. I don't care—it's from Elvis! No one else I know has one! She was surprised—kinda happy—that I'm moving. She said she hopes I will be happy.

JUNE, 1961   Saw "Wild in the Country" with Elvis. It was OK. Not too much singing. Elvis is in love with 3 different girls and can't decide which one he wants to marry. His acting was good. I like the part where he was drunk and went to see his psychiatrist. It was funny! He had been dating Tuesday Weld before they made this movie together and they're dating again. I don't like her. She's not his type.

AUGUST, 1961   We moved to Merrillville. It's in the country. There's a grocery store, 2 churches, a bowling alley, a restaurant, Dairy Queen, a bakery, a drug store where the post office is, US 30 Drag Strip, and the Y and W drive in theater. The subdivision is called Turkey Creek. Our house is the first one built on our block. People choose a house they want from model homes. Ours is a tri-level. It has a basement with a den, half bath, and laundry area. The main floor has a living room, dining room, and kitchen. The kitchen has a built in oven and matching stove. All the rooms are carpeted. There are 3 bedrooms and 2 bathrooms upstairs. My room is so big. I got new furniture. I love it. Mom won't let me put Elvis pics on the walls, but I have one big one on the closet door. Elvis has lots of new records out. My favorite is "It's Now or Never." Saw "Blue Hawaii." I love this movie! Funny, lots of songs and beautiful Hawaii! I want to visit there one day. Now Elvis is dating Joan Blackman. Guess he's fickle.

SEPTEMBER 3, 1961   School started. It's much smaller than Lew Wallace. It is one building with 3 floors. Grades 1-8. Next year I'll go to the high school. Kids are so much nicer here. Most of the parents are doctors and lawyers. No one makes fun of me, and they like Elvis. I'm so glad we moved.

OCTOBER 21, 1961   Got another letter from Elvis! My heart is pounding! This one says: "Hello Again, It's been a long time since I wrote you. But as you know I've had a pretty busy summer and spent most of it in Florida filming "Pioneer Go Home" my latest movie. The Florida sunshine was great, and believe me I got plenty of it, since we did practically all the filming in Crystal River. I am at home now in Memphis enjoying a few weeks rest and some of the quieter things like football, TV, and being with my family. I'll return to Calif. in a few weeks to start my next movie. It's always nice to know you're thinking of me. Keep your nice letters coming I'll be writing again soon. But for a while I'll say Bye Bye. Sincerely Yours, Elvis." I still can't believe all this is happening to me! No one that I know can believe this, either. He knows me, has my address. Maybe I'll send my telephone number in my next letter.

DECEMBER 4, 1961   Christmas card from Elvis! White background with the Nativity scene and inside in gold. "May the joy and peace of Christmas be with you today and all through the year. Elvis Presley and Family." Love it!

May THE JOY AND PEACE OF *Christmas*

BE WITH YOU TODAY

AND ALL THROUGH THE YEAR

ELVIS PRESLEY AND FAMILY

Dear Sandy:

    I just boarded the airplane here in Honolulu to head back to Hollywood and thought you might be interested to know what I've been doing lately.

    For the past month we have been filming "Blue Hawaii" over on the Hawaiian Islands. The scenery there is just gorgeous. The weather was always nice and everyone was so friendly, I really enjoyed working there.

    After completing the rest of the film in Hollywood, I will return home — to Memphis around the first of June.

    I see the stewardess serving dinner, so I'd better sign off for now.

    Take good care of yourself and write soon!

                    Sincerely,
                      Elvis Presley

Hello Again,

It's been a long time since I wrote you.

But as you know I've had a pretty busy summer. And spent most of it in Florida filming "Follow That Dream" My latest Movie.

The Florida sunshine was great, And believe me I got plenty of it, Since we did practically all the filming in Crystal River.

I am at home now, in Memphis enjoying a few weeks rest And some of the sweeter things like football, T.V. And being with my family.

I'll Return to Calif in a few weeks to start my next Movie.

Its always nice to know you're thinking of me. Keep your nice letters coming. I'll be writing again soon But for awhile I'll say Bye Bye

Sincerely Yours
Elvis.

1962

JANUARY 8, 1962   Elvis' 27th birthday. I hope he got my card on time. I dreamed I went to a carnival and met Elvis. The rides were running and music played. Elvis walked to me and shook my hand. I couldn't see his face, only his black shoes! I don't understand that.

JULY 6, 1962   Vic, our family friend, is going to Memphis next month with his daughter, Little Sandy. They know I love Elvis, so Vic asked Mom and Dad if I could go. They said yes! I can't believe it! I'm so happy! I'll see Graceland! I'm praying Elvis will be home and I'll meet him! We'll stay with Vic's nephew, Tony, and his wife, Dee, and their baby, Gina. We'll leave on Aug. 8! I can't wait!

AUGUST 6, 1962   Only 2 days before we leave! My clothes are packed. Mom made me some slacks and skirts and tops to take. I keep wishing on every star I see and on my lucky penny. I pray all the time that Elvis will be home. It will be a dream come true. Hedda Hopper reported in her magazine that he is finished filming. He might be there. Marilyn Monroe committed suicide today. I cried. She was pretty and a good actress.

AUGUST 8, 1962   We left home around 10:00 AM. The scenery is pretty. I dozed off and on. It was a long trip. Got to Memphis at 11:45 PM. It took an hour to find Tony's house. It's a new house and very pretty. We introduced ourselves and went straight to bed. Little Sandy shared a bed with me. She kept me awake until 3:30 AM.

AUGUST 9, 1962   Little Sandy started pestering me to get up at 6:30. I got up at 8:30. I couldn't stand it anymore. Tony and Dee took us to meet her parent's, the Bomprazos, at their home. We met Lisa, Dee's cousin from Alabama, and Tootie, Dee's sister, who is deaf. They are both Elvis fans. Tootie attends a special school and is learning to talk as well as use sign language. She grabbed my transistor radio, turned it up, and put her hand on top. Dee said that's how she "hears" the music and words! Tony has an article from the newspaper stating how Tootie loves Elvis and listens to his songs.

We visited Vic's dad's grave and went to Forrest Hills Cemetery to see Elvis' mother's grave. In front of the grave is a 6'-8' white marble cross. The stone says: Gladys Love Smith Presley Beloved Wife of Vernon Presley and Mother of Elvis Aron Presley   April 25, 1912-August 14, 1958. She Was The Sunshine Of Our Home."

    We took pictures of it, and I touched it because I knew Elvis did. We went to Whitehaven, a suburb of Memphis, to see Graceland. I was surprised that it is so close to the highway. I thought it would be off by itself on a big ranch, like in the movies. There was an 8' or 10' cement or rock fence all around it. Cars were parked in front of the fence. Tony parked the car. We got out and walked to an empty field on the right hand side to take pictures. I saw the barn in the upper right hand side of the property, but I knew my camera would not take a good picture. I wanted to save film for pictures of Elvis. We went to the gates. It had Elvis' image on both gates, and they were open. Elvis' uncle Travis, the gateman, talked to us and some other people. I asked if it was true that there were tours of the mansion. Travis said, "Yes- when Elvis is not home. But he's home and sleeping now. He gets up about 2:00 in the afternoon." I was hysterical! I heard myself screaming, "He's here! Elvis is home!" Lisa and I hugged each other and danced in a circle, laughing and screaming. Tony asked Travis if he knew if Elvis would be down. Travis didn't know for sure, but Elvis signed autographs and posed for pictures yesterday. The trees were in full bloom and hid the mansion, so I couldn't take pictures. Travis took my camera and drove up to take some for me. Vic likes to tease me about Elvis.

He asked a guy standing next to him if he could believe us being so crazy. The guy looked at him and said, "I want to see him as much as they do!" Vic was shocked! When Travis returned with our cameras, Tony told Travis I came from Ind. to meet Elvis and gave him the newspaper article about Tootie. Travis took the article and Tony's phone number and promised to show them to Elvis. Elvis' black Cadillac sat in front of the mansion. It has a snack bar, TV, phone, etc. Horses were running in a fenced area. On the left of Graceland stands Graceland Christian Church. It was part of the property Elvis purchased. He donated the land to the congregation. We'll go to church there Sun. I collected some leaves as a souvenir. We left Graceland to have lunch at Vannucci's, the restaurant where Vernon Presley ate lunch every day. I was too excited to eat. Tony made me a promise that before I left Memphis, he would personally introduce me to Elvis--even if we had to stay in Memphis a few days longer. We went to the drive in to see "Blue Hawaii" and "G.I. Blues." They and "Jailhouse Rock" are my favorite movies.

AUGUST 10, 1962   Tony took us for a tour of downtown Memphis. It's beautiful and has so much history. I fell in love with it. Saw the Mississippi River, riverboats, Beale St., Sun Record Co., and the theater where Elvis worked as an usher in high school. I was surprised how nice everyone was—smiling and nodding at us. When a colored person would walk toward us on the sidewalk, he or she would step out into the street to let us pass. Strange signs for drinking fountains were labeled WHITES ONLY and COLOREDS ONLY. The restroom signs were labeled WHITE WOMEN (or men) and COLORED WOMEN (or men). I didn't understand it. When we were in the car leaving, Tony explained things to me. I learned a new word today: segregation.

AUGUST 11, 1962   Went to Sardis Lake in Mississippi. Elvis takes his boat there a lot to swim and ski. We had a picnic, swam, and danced to the radio. I kept looking around to see if Elvis would show up, but he didn't. It was hot. We had a good time.

We left late in the afternoon and went to the Bomprazo's house to clean up and eat dinner. When we sat down to eat, Vic said, "Should we tell them now?" The others said no we should wait. I asked what they were talking about. Tony said he would tell us after we finished eating. I wasn't hungry but I ate a little pasta. The phone rang while we were eating. Mr. Bomprazo, a policeman, answered it, talked for a minute, hung up, and returned to the table with a big grin on his face. He walked to me, put his hands on my shoulders, and said, "When I was on patrol today, I saw a car stalled on Poplar Blvd. I stopped to help. Four guys got out of the car to help push it to the side of the road. It took about an hour to get the car started. The driver's window rolled down. The driver was Elvis! He offered to pay me for my help. I said no, it was the Christian thing to do. Elvis insisted that I give him my name and address so he could send a check to me. I refused. I told Elvis about you girls and how much you want to meet him. Elvis asked for my 'phone number and wrote it down. He's renting the fairgrounds tonight and you girls are invited. He said someone would call with the time. That was one of Elvis' friends who just called. Elvis said to be there at midnight tonight."

Lisa and I looked at each other in disbelief. Dee signed the message to Tootie. Everyone was so excited! I couldn't eat any more. My stomach was churning. I was crying. It was unbelievable.

The fairgrounds was down the street. There was no hurry to leave. We left at 10:30 PM. A small crowd was there. I was afraid we wouldn't get in. Travis drove up. Tony walked to him, talked, and motioned to us to join them. Travis smiled and said he was glad we could come. He showed us where to stand and wait. He assured us he would get us in. I thanked him. We waited for what seemed like forever. After about ½ hour later, Elvis' black Caddy drove up. My heart was pounding.

AUGUST 12, 1962   The gates opened at 12:15 AM. Travis and the Memphis Mafia stood there watching the crowd. A loud voice yelled out: "No cameras. No pictures. No autographs. Ride the rides and eat all you want. Everything is free. Enjoy yourself, but don't bother Elvis, or you will be asked to leave." I took a deep breath. I wouldn't bother him; I just wanted to SEE him! As we entered the gates, I was in shock! This was the carnival I had been dreaming about! Everything was exactly the same! Vic said, "There's Elvis—over there by his car." Tony walked to

Elvis, introduced himself, and led Elvis to us and said, "Elvis, this is Sandy. She came all the way from Indiana to meet you." Elvis said, "Hi, Sandy. That's so nice of you." I was so scared. I couldn't look into his face! I stared down at his black, shiny shoes just like in my dreams! I stuck my hand out to shake his. His handshake was firm but gentle. I got the chills! Tony introduced the rest of our group and I looked up at Elvis. He was so pale but even more handsome than in the movies. He's much taller than I imagined. He wore a yellow, unbuttoned shirt, tight black slacks, and a motorcycle hat. He smiled and was so friendly and talked about the hot weather. We thanked him for being so nice to us. He thanked US, told us to enjoy ourselves, and he would talk to us later. We walked away and rode some rides. I kept going back to see him. He was so nervous. I bet he smoked 2 packs of cigarettes. I stood alone by his car and looked at him. He glanced over at me, smiled, and began walking toward me! Some guys crowded him. They asked stupid questions about Hollywood and stayed so close to him that he could hardly move. He looked at me several times. He smiled and tried again to walk to me, but the guys stepped in front of him. He smiled at me again, shrugged his shoulders, and stayed in the middle of the crowd. He looked disappointed. I know I was! He wanted to get away, but he didn't ask them to leave. He was very friendly and talked for a long time. Guys asked for autographs. Tony spotted me and walked to me. He told me to get an autograph. I got my school autograph book and a pencil from my purse. I walked toward Elvis, but the guys blocked me. I froze. Tony told me to hurry. I looked up at Elvis and all the guys surrounding me. I couldn't move. Tony pushed me to Elvis. I managed to stop before I ran into him, but my arm was touching his. "You almost made me run into him!" I yelled at Tony. Elvis turned his head and looked down at me and smiled. Tony walked up to me. "Elvis, can she have your autograph, please? I have to be at work in a couple hours, so we have to leave." Elvis nodded, took the pencil and book, signed his name, smiled at me, and returned the items to me. I whispered a thank you. He smiled and said, "Thank you." Tony gently grabbed me and we all walked to Tony's car. I was in heaven! I stared at the autograph, touched my hand and started to cry. I was happy and sad. I wanted to stay longer and talk to Elvis and maybe get a picture. But, I was lucky to have been with him for a short while. I'll never forget this night!

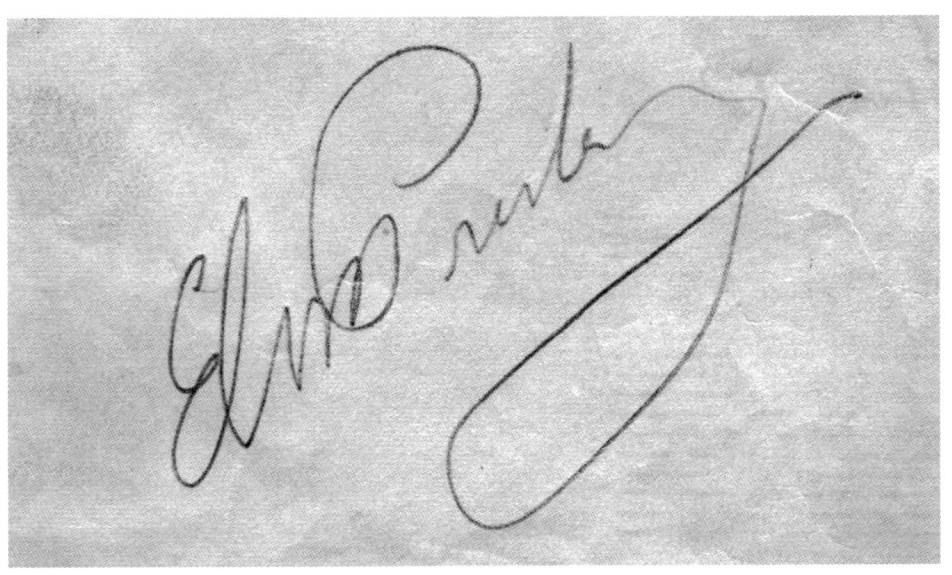

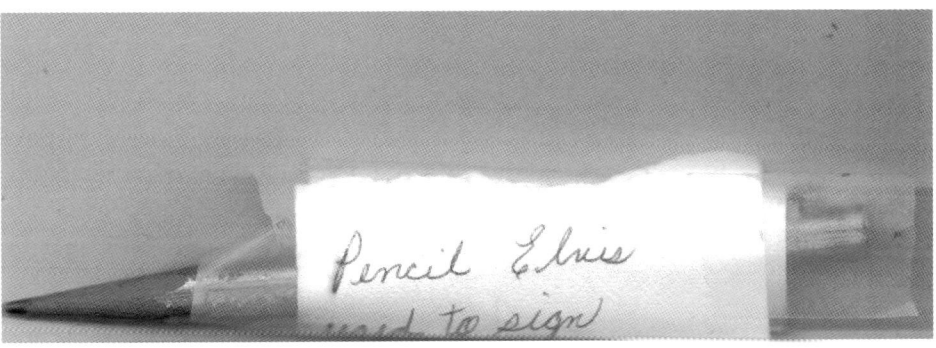

AUGUST 13, 1962   No one got up for church. I felt guilty, but we were so tired. Louie, Dees' cousin took us to a park where Elvis plays football. He didn't show, so we went horseback riding. It was my first time to ride a horse alone. It was so hot! The horse kept bending down to drink. I almost fell into the lake! Louie saved me. I have a crush on him. He looks like Elvis. He was jealous that I saw Elvis last night.

AUGUST 14, 1962   Went by Graceland. Elvis didn't come out. I left a note with Travis to give to Elvis. I thanked Elvis for letting us go to the fairgrounds. I told him how happy I was to meet him. I asked if I could meet with him privately. I would love to have my picture taken with him. A kiss would be nice, too.

AUGUST 15, 1962   A newspaper article said Elvis and Anita Wood broke up. She wants to get married, but he doesn't. I wondered why she wasn't with him the other night. Maybe that's why he was so nervous.

AUGUST 16, 1962   Our last day in Memphis. Went to Graceland to say goodbye to Travis. Elvis hadn't been out for a couple nights. Dee and Tony had a BBQ going away party for us. We danced, had fireworks. It was so nice. Wish I could stay here. I made up my mind that I will live in Memphis some day.

AUGUST 17, 1962   Woke up at 8:00, packed our stuff, drove by Graceland, and we were on our way home. I looked at Graceland until it was out of sight. I cried. Was glad to see Mom and Dad and even Tony. I couldn't stop talking about all that happened. Mom said it's OK for me to invite my friends over in a couple days for a party and talk about the trip. Felt good to be in my own bed. I dreamed about Elvis.

SEPTEMBER 1, 1962   Last weekend before school starts. Got a bunch of girls together to see Elvis' movies "Kid Galahad," "Girls! Girls! Girls!", and "Follow That Dream" at the Y and W drive in. I liked "Follow That Dream" the best. We sang along with all the songs and had fun watching some kids making out in their cars. We talked about how I met Elvis; we couldn't get that out of our heads.

SEPTEMBER 4, 1962   First day of school. Glad all my friends and I had the same lunch hour. As we sat in our regular spot to eat, I saw a dark haired girl sitting alone. She looked sad and scared. My heart ached for her. I yelled to her to join us. I introduced all of us: Patty, Renee, Connie, Pat and me. She smiled and sat down. Her name is Bonnie. She just moved from Ft. Wayne. I explained I had just met Elvis; her face brightened! She is an Elvis fan! I knew we would all get along. We talked about Elvis until the bell rang.

DECEMBER 4, 1962   I got a Christmas card from Elvis!! It's pretty blue, has Santa in his sleigh and the reindeer in the yard of Graceland. "At Christmas...We send warm greetings to you as a friend and we share with you some views of Graceland...our home." The Presleys   I unfolded the card. Beautiful shots of Graceland!! It made my day so much better.

DECEMBER 25, 1962   Got a stereo record player, records, and clothes for Christmas. Sad news: we are moving back to Hobart! I hate that! I wish I was 16. I'd quit school and get a job. I won't be with my friends. Bonnie is my best friend. She comes to my house every day after school. It will be long distance to call on the phone. Mom says we can have PJ parties and spend weekends together. It won't be the same.

DECEMBER 31, 1962   We moved. The house is old and cold. My bedroom is so small I can hardly move. My stereo is in the dining room. At least there is a door I can close for some privacy. Two bedrooms are upstairs. I'm alone on the main floor. The TV is in the basement. I want to run away. I dreamed that Elvis died. I woke up crying. I felt so helpless and sad. I hope he's ok.

1963

JANUARY 8, 1963   Elvis' 28th birthday.

FEBUARY 4, 1963   I got another letter from Elvis! "Dear Sandy, Time has flown by and we are now facing a new year. I want to wish you a late but prosperous New Year. I am sorry I haven't gotten around to it sooner, but I'm sure you understand how rushed I am around Christmas time. Hope you had a wonderful Christmas and I sincerely hope this New Year will be the most prosperous and happiest one you have ever had. I want to thank you for your loyal support and your nice cards and letters for the year of 1962, and all the others in the past. My new picture I recently finished is called "It Happened at the World's Fair" and is supposed to be released around Easter. I hope you like it. I had a wonderful Christmas, birthday, and New Year at home with my folks. I am now leaving for the West Coast to start filming a new picture which as of now is named "Holiday in Acapulco", part of it will be filmed in Acapulco, Mexico. I hope to be back home in Memphis sometime in April for a few days rest between pictures. As I am pressed for time, I guess I'd better run now. Keep writing your wonderful letters and I will answer you every chance I get. Best wishes to you and yours. Sincerely yours, Elvis Presley"

MARCH 16, 1963   My 15th birthday. I'll be sweet 16 next year. We celebrated with cake and gifts. Bonnie came over for the weekend. We played cards, danced, and talked. Glad we can spend weekends together to catch up on everything. She got her driver's permit. She can get her license in 6 months. We'll be able to cruise around. Can't wait to get my license.

APRIL, 1963   Saw "It Happened at the World's Fair." Funny. Good songs.

JUNE 18, 1963   Our Sunday school class is going to Riverview Park in Chicago tomorrow. It will be fun to be with real friends and ride all the rides.

JUNE 19, 1963   Woke up so sick. Cramps and throwing up. Couldn't go to Riverview. Stayed in bed all day.

Dear ~~Wendy~~

Time has flown by and we are now facing a new year. I want to wish you a late but a prosperous new year. I am sorry I haven't gotten around to it sooner, but I'm sure you understand how rushed I am around Christmas time. Hope you had a wonderful Christmas and I sincerely hope this new year will be the most prosperous and happiest one you have ever had.

I want to thank you for your loyal support and for your nice cards and letters for the year of 1962, and all others in the past.

My new picture I recently finished, is called "It Happened At The World's Fair" and is suppose to be released around Easter. I hope you like it.

I had a wonderful Christmas, Birthday and New Year at home with my folks. I am now leaving for the West Coast to start filming a new picture which as of now is named "Holiday In Acupulo", part of it will be filmed in Acupulo, Mexico. I hope to be back home in Memphis sometime in April for a few days rest between pictures. As I am pressed for time, I guess I'd better run now. Keep writing your wonderful letters and I will answer you every chance I get. Best wishes to you and yours.

          Sincerely Yours,

          Elvis Presley

JUNE 20, 1963   I am so sick. I stayed home from church. It's Father's Day. I can't eat. The pain is so bad. Mom and Dad took me to the hospital. I was admitted. Doctors think it might be my appendix. A surgeon will see me tomorrow.

JUNE 21, 1963   I had exploratory surgery. Doctors found a 3 lb. cyst in my abdomen. It broke as they tried to remove it. They don't know where it came from. It is not cancerous. Doctor said if I had gone to Riverview yesterday, the cyst would have broken and I would have died.

JUNE 29, 1963   I got to go home. I can't dance or do anything strenuous. Have to be careful not to rip the stitches. The scar is below my navel all across my body. Looks awful, but no one will ever see it. Get stitches out next week.

JUNE 30, 1963   Mom and Dad told me they found a house for rent in Merrillville! It's on Broadway just a mile from school. I am so happy! It's a big house with a porch the entire front and left side. Small kitchen, 3 bedrooms, 1 bath, huge living room and dining room . Huge back yard with a grape vine separating the property. Also has a big brick BBQ pit. Two car garage. I love it!

SEPTEMBER 8, 1963   School started. No classes with any of my friends, but we have the same lunch hour. The kids are still all nice. Rumors are that Priscilla is living in Memphis with Vernon and Dee. Elvis and Ann Margret are filming a movie, "Viva Las Vegas." They are dating. I saw her in "Bye Bye Birdie" and "State Fair." Everyone thinks she's so pretty and talented. I don't see anything special about her. Some reporters are saying Elvis will marry her. I hope not. He should marry Priscilla—she's been waiting for him for a long time.

NOVEMBER 11, 1963   President Kennedy was assassinated in Dallas, TX! I was in Business Math class when it was announced on the loud speaker. We were all in shock! Everyone was crying! We were immediately dismissed from school. The news keeps showing him being shot. They were riding in a convertible. Mrs. Kennedy tried to get out of the car for safety. Vice President Lyndon Johnson was sworn in as President. It's a very sad day for America.

NOVEMBER 12, 1963   All schools, government agencies,

everything-- except a few selected drugstores--are all closed by law. The only thing on TV is about the Kennedys. Nothing will reopen until after the funeral. Lee Harvey Oswald was arrested for the shooting.

DECEMBER 25, 1963   Can't believe this year is nearly over. Hope things get better. The family came for dinner again. I love it when we all get together. Exchanged gifts and stuff. Tony has grown over 2 ft this year! So strange to have to look up to him. We lit the fire place. Beautiful tree. Played Elvis' Christmas songs. Hope it's warmer tomorrow so Bonnie can pick me and the other girls up and go cruising. We like to tease the boys. So much fun.

1964

JANUARY 8, 1964   Elvis' 29th birthday.

MARCH 16, 1964   My Sweet 16th birthday! I am so excited! I can get my driver's permit in 6 months. Grandpa Pupek died. Mom and Dad went to Baltimore for the funeral. Vic got permission from Mom and Dad to have my friends over for a party. We had pizza, pop, and cake. We danced and had a good time. Saw "Kissin' Cousins." It's funny. Elvis plays look alike cousins! Cool!

April 4, 1964   Went to see "Viva Las Vegas". Funny movie, a lot of singing and dancing. Great because Elvis starred, but I didn't like Ann Margret. She's stuck up and phony. Glad they're not dating any more. She and Tuesday Weld are the only two co-stars of his that I didn't like.

MAY 1, 1964   Not much happening. Babysitting some, dating a little, doing well in school. I'd like to be a writer. I write a lot of poems and some of my stories have been printed in the Pirate school newspaper. Go to see Elvis' movies, but they're not as good as the older ones. He has many new records, but no #1 hits except "Return to Sender." He's still good. Magazines say he's tired of the movies and wants to go back touring and singing. I still write him. He doesn't seem to be very happy any more. He is more handsome every day. I pray he will find happiness. The Beatles, a band from England, is having one hit record after another. I'm tired of hearing them. I don't like them.

JUNE, 1964   Elvis' new movies "Roustabout" with Barbara Stanwyck and "Girl Happy" are out. Songs and girls are the plot.

SEPTEMBER 16, 1964   I passed my drivers' test! Dad has been taking me out to practice for a long time. I had trouble parking, but the examiner helped me. His only complaint was that I drive too slow.

1965

MARCH 16, 1965   My 17th birthday. The family was over. The war in Viet Nam is getting worse. More of our GIs are killed every day. The government opened a special P.O. Box for our guys there. I told our Sunday school class about it. Nearly everyone agreed to write letters to the guys to show our support and prayers. I will send one every week. If it helps brighten someone's day, that will be a blessing from God. Elvis' movies "Tickle Me" and "Harum Scarum" were OK.

APRIL 14, 1965   Received letters from 3 soldiers. Jimmy from Hawaii, Larry from Iowa, and John from Colorado. I promised to write them weekly until they return home. They are all very nice. They are scared and lonely. I pray for them every night.

1966

MARCH 16, 1966   My 18th birthday. I am an A and B honor roll student for the 3rd year in a row. Thinking about college, but I don't want to leave home. The only soldier I'm still writing is John. The others went home and stopped writing. Wish this war was over.

JUNE 3, 1966   Graduation Day. Happy but sad. I think we all cried. My open house will be in the church basement. We had 105 students, the largest class in Merrillville history! Mom and Dad got me a used Plymouth for my gift! I can't wait to drive it!

JUNE 4, 1966   Dad took me out in my car. It's a stick shift. I'm having problems getting it in the right gears. Dad doesn't understand why I can't get the hang of it.

JUNE 6, 1966   Dad traded the car for a Ford. It's automatic! I can drive any where! So happy!

JUNE 12, 1966   All my family and friends from school came to my party. Got lots of nice gifts and money. I decided not to go to college. Maybe next year. I want to be a writer. Grandma and Grandpa went to Italy. They asked me to go. They want me to meet Gino and marry him. I don't want to move to Italy. Mom and Dad are building a new house in Chapel Manor. We'll move soon. My picture was on the front page of the Gary Post Tribune. Patty and I had a contest to see who could grow the longest fingernails. I won! 1- 1/2" long!

JULY 13, 1966   A man had his picture in the paper with his 1 ¾" fingernail!

July 14, 1966   We moved into our new house. 3 bedrooms, 3 baths, den, sunken living room, huge kitchen. I love it.

AUGUST, 1966   Elvis' new movies: "Paradise Hawaiian Style" and "Spinout." They are all OK. I like a lot of the songs.

DECEMBER 24, 1966   Got a Christmas card from Elvis ! A beautiful picture of him. He's wearing a red jacket, jeans, and a white shirt. The message is: "Seasons Greetings Elvis and the Colonel" 1966

DECEMBER 31, 1966   My pic with the fingernail was in the paper again as interesting happenings in 1966!

1967

APRIL 8, 1967   Grandpa Falcetta died today of pneumonia. I have never hurt so much in my life. I loved him so much. He used to hold me on his lap and tell me about Italy and New York. I put my head on his chest and listened to his heartbeat. I can never do that again. The Italian and U.S. government won't allow his body to be brought here for at least a year. Grandma will stay in Italy until then.

APRIL 30, 1967   I got a job with DNJ Printers. I work in the shipping dept. I went to Lew Wallace with one of the girls there. They're not very friendly, but I do my job and try to be friendly.

MAY 1, 1967   When I got up to go to work, Mom told me Elvis was married last night in Las Vegas! I listened to the radio to see to whom. It was Pris! I sighed for relief that it was Pris and not Ann Margret. It hurts to know he's married, but I'm so glad it's her and not Ann Margret! I cried off and on all day. The news keeps showing pictures of them cutting the cake and kissing. I hope Elvis is happy. I know he has been so lonely.

MAY 18, 1967   I've been sick for several weeks. I have gallstones and must have surgery to remove them. They also found a cyst in my left breast. Doctor wants to do both surgeries at once. If I have cancer, they will remove my breast. I'm so scared. The doctor gave me pills to calm my nerves.

JUNE 3, 1967   I had surgery. Thank God, there was no cancer!

JUNE 15, 1967   Went to see the doctor. He told me I have to quit my job. It's too strenuous. He increased nerve pills to 3 a day. I don't want to go to college. John still writes. He leaves Nam next year and will be on leave for quite a while. He re-upped in the Army for 4 more years. He'll go to Germany.

JULY 12, 1967   Dad agreed to pay for me to take writing courses by mail. That's what I want to do—write. I've written several scripts for Elvis, but never got them to him. I decided I want to go to Hollywood or Memphis to give them to him. I sent him some of my poems, but no response. Saw "Easy Come Easy Go." Also "Double Trouble," "Clambake." They're all almost the same. If Elvis wasn't in them, I don't think I'd pay to see them.

OCTOBER 12, 1967   Elvis and Priscilla are expecting a baby! I'm so happy for them. I hope it's a boy; Elvis is the last male in the Presley family. He loves kids. He'll be a good father.

SEPTEMBER 6, 1967   Bonnie and her sister, Marti, moved to Ft. Wayne. They want me to go with them, but I can't because I'm healing from surgery and my nerves are too bad. Actually, I'm afraid I'll be home sick that far away from home. I hope they find jobs and happiness. I'll miss Bon.

DECEMBER 22, 1967   Bonnie and Marti came home for the holidays. They both have good jobs and like being back in Ft. Wayne. They made vows to marry preachers. Marti met a guy studying to preach and they are engaged! I think Bonnie is happy and jealous about that. She applied to attend Ozark Bible College and was accepted! She starts classes Jan. 12, 1968. She's so excited and wants me to go. If I go to any college, it will be Lincoln Christian in Illinois.

DECEMBER 25, 1967   I love Christmas! Bon and I spent time together with both our families. She and Marti will leave tomorrow for Ft. Wayne. She has to give notice to her boss that she's quitting. I pray she's doing the right thing. Her grades weren't that great in high school. I know college courses will be much harder, and I won't be there to help her. She's mainly going for her MRS. Degree. I hope she finds the right guy. She loves the Lord and wants to serve Him. She deserves the best.

1968

FEBRUARY 1, 1968   Elvis and Priscilla had a baby girl! Her name is Lisa Marie. She's a little doll. Elvis is so proud and happy. I'm glad he found true love and joy.

MARCH 16, 1968   My 20th birthday. I've been babysitting and working on my writing. I've gotten all A's on my assignments. John is leaving Nam in July. He'll be on leave for 30 days and he wants to meet me.

Mom and Dad think he wants to marry me. We've never mentioned love or marriage.

APRIL 4, 1968   As we watched Martin Luther King's speech in Memphis on TV, I blurted out: "He'd better watch himself. He might get shot." The newscast was interrupted to report that Mr. King had just been shot! I was in shock! Don't know why I said that. He died shortly afterward.

APRIL 15, 1968   There was an earthquake in Italy! Thank God, Grandma is safe. The government is forcing her to fly home. She's terrified.

April 18, 1968   Grandma made the trip safely. She can't believe she got here so fast. They always traveled by boat. Grandpa's body will be sent here next week.

APRIL 25, 1968   Grandpa's body is in the States. Arrangements for burial tomorrow afternoon.

APRIL 26, 1968   Such a sad day. I couldn't stop crying. Glad Grandma is here.

JUNE 1, 1968   Bonnie is home. She barely passed her classes and she can't afford to continue her studies. We're discussing moving to Memphis to find jobs and husbands. We want to start new lives. Our parents say it's too dangerous for girls to live alone. I'm determined to move to Memphis! Everyone is so nice there. Bon and I are praying about it.

AUGUST 1, 1968   Bon and I decided to move to Memphis. Dee and Tony agreed to let us stay with them for a few days and look for jobs.

AUGUST 8, 1968   Bon and I drove to Memphis in her new Chevy Nova. It's a nice car. The gas pedal is different and up so high that I can't reach it. We had a safe trip. Had dinner with Dee and family. They have a son, Tony, Jr.

AUGUST 9, 1968   Job hunting didn't go well. No one wants to hire us until we get a place to live. We left applications anyway.

AUGUST 10, 1968   Bon and I went to Tupelo, Miss. to see the house and town where Elvis was born. It is smaller than Mom's home town in KY. Elvis remembered that there was no place for kids to play, so he had a park built. It's so nice of him to do that. I'm proud of him. Went to Gladys' grave and took pictures. As we drove to Graceland, Bon said she likes it here and does want to move. I'm glad! The gates were closing when we arrived at Graceland, but since no one else was there, the guards let us in. One was Elvis' uncle Vester, Vernon's brother. The other was a cousin. Vester said Elvis hired his family and friends to work for him, because he remembered all they had done for him when he was growing up. Elvis is not home. He's filming a Christmas special to be aired on TV in December!

We asked to go closer to take pictures. Vester drove us to the mansion in a golf cart. My heart pounded. We were allowed on the porch. He took pics of us. The columns and lion statues were beautiful. I sat on the steps and looked toward the highway. It was so peaceful. I felt Elvis' presence the way I did when I first met him. The window shutters were painted green. Then came the shock! There were black steel bars over the windows! Vester said they are for security, just like the barbed wire on top of the fence. Poor Elvis! A prisoner in his own home! The driveway formed a circle in front of the mansion and joined with the main drive and back down to the street. I told Vester we are planning to move to Memphis. He wished us luck and said he hoped to see us again.

AUGUST 11, 1968   Mom called. John is coming! We packed and left for home. I hated to leave Memphis, but it's exciting to think about meeting John. On the way home, a woman ran a stop sign and hit Bon's car on the side. The police were called and came right away. Tickets were written against the lady stating she was the guilty party. All the reports were written up. No one was hurt. Bon's car could be driven. It isn't even a month old. I felt so sorry for her. I kept joking around to try to cheer her up. Thank God the rest of the trip went safely! Mom and Dad weren't upset that I didn't find a job. They keep teasing me about getting married to John. I told them we have to see how things go. Sometimes, people don't get along in person. I honestly don't want to move to Germany, and I don't think John would want us to be separated IF we get married.

AUGUST 14, 1968   Mom drove me to O'Hare airport to get John. He's nice looking and so tall. We are both shy, so Mom did most of the talking on the way home. He is very nice. Mom cooked a delicious dinner for us. She and Dad liked John right away. I never had a guy spend the night in our house, and being right next to my room is really scary! I'm afraid to make a sound.

AUGUST 15, 1968   Went to the Science and Industry museum in Chicago. Took lots of pictures of us. We are going to Grandma's tomorrow for spaghetti dinner.

AUGUST 16, 1968   John and Grandma got along really well. He loves Italian food, and she loves to cook. So glad they like each other. Grandma seemed so happy for me. I'm glad she's back home.

AUGUST 17, 1968   We took John to O'Hare. Mom took the wrong turn, so we were almost late for the flight. We had to rush to get to the plane, but we made it. It was sad kissing John goodbye. He has my phone number and will call. I'll miss him. I really like him.

AUGUST 18, 1968   Got a call from my biological father that Grandma passed away last night. I can't believe it! She was so happy and spry. We were just together. God, how can this be? She was reading her Bible when she died. I know she and Grandpa are in Heaven. I'll see them again. But it hurts.

AUGUST 25, 1968   We buried Grandma today next to Grandpa. Their plots were purchased when Grandpa was brought home. I know Grandma was so lonely without him. She would only wear black for mourning. She missed him too much. John has been calling every day to see how I am. He was shocked to hear about Grandma. He wants to get married. I told him I can't right now. He understands. He leaves for Germany in a few weeks. We promised to stay in touch. I miss him, too. But I need my family too much now.

SEPTEMBER, 1968   Elvis movies "Stay Away, Joe," "Speedway," and "Live a Little, Love a Little" are released. He doesn't seem to enjoy the acting as much as he did. Rumor has it he wants to quit movies and start touring and singing. But, he gets $1million per movie. So….

DECEMBER 3, 1968   Elvis' Singer Sewing Machine Christmas Special was on. Man, is he fantastic! So thin. Even more handsome. Wore a black, leather suit and kidded about how hot it was. The stage was in the middle of a group of lucky of girls. He talked to the girls, the band, joked around about his lip and his shaky legs from his beginning performances. He sang most of his first songs "Love Me Tender," "All Shook Up," and "Heartbreak Hotel." Sang some new songs as well. His voice is even better now! He sang gospel songs. The last song was "If I Can Dream." Col. Parker didn't want him to sing it. Says it's too controversial. He wanted Elvis to only sing Christmas songs. The producers asked Elvis what HE wanted to do. Elvis wanted to do what the producers said. It started a bunch of trouble between Elvis and the Col. Elvis and the producers won! The show was the highest rated special ever shown. I was so excited about the show that I got sick. Cried myself to sleep like I used to when I first fell in love with Elvis. I'd love to see and hear him sing in person one day.

1969

JUNE, 1969   Elvis' movies and records have not been selling well. The movies all have the same plot. Some good songs, but nothing special. His last movies "Charro!" "The Trouble With Girls" and "Change of Habit" are ok. His contracts with the movie studios are finished. I wonder what the Col. will do for him now.

JULY, 1969   Letters from John are getting farther apart. I've gone out with a few guys, but nothing serious. I'm still writing and working at odd jobs. Bonnie is a bookkeeper at KMART. She likes it.

DECEMBER, 1969   Elvis started singing in Las Vegas. He's getting $1 million a month! Everyone is raving about his performance. He's matured in attitude and his voice is smoother. He's singing songs from the beginning of his career and a lot of new ones. RCA is taping the shows and selling the records. Guess the Col. decided the money is better than the movies. Some say Elvis is having money problems. He's buying cars for his friends and family and not keeping track of the funds.

1970

AUGUST 16, 1970   Elvis is being sued for paternity by a girl named Patricia Parker. I don't believe Elvis would be unfaithful to Priscilla. They love each other too much, and they have sweet Lisa Marie.

SEPTEMBER 1, 1970   Elvis was found innocent of the paternity suit. I knew it! Started working for Wards catalog store in Crown Point. Love it! Everyone is so nice; they're all older ladies and spoil me.

1971

FEBRUARY 2, 1971   The Apollo astronauts landed on the moon!

FEBRUARY 5, 1971   The astronauts WALKED on the moon! So exciting!

MAY 12, 1971   Hazel introduced me to Danny. He, his son, and daughter live with his mom. His wife left for another man. He's a welder.

JUNE-OCTOBER, 1971   Danny and I are serious about each other. I bought used furniture for us to start out with. I love his kids, and they love me. He has been traveling in order to find work. He's in Texas now working. He filed desertion as the reason for divorce. He has to wait a year to give his wife the right to claim for custody of the kids. We will have to be patient. I keep praying there will be no problems.

OCTOBER 10, 1971   Elvis is going on a nationwide tour, but not in Chicago!

DECEMBER 24, 1971   Danny came home for Christmas. He and the kids spent a lot of time with me. He gave me a beautiful jewelry box for Christmas. I kept looking for an engagement ring in each drawer, but there wasn't one. Had services at church. Danny wouldn't go. He wanted to be with his family and friends and get drunk. As I sat in the choir, tears came to my eyes. I thought about how I could have been with Danny. Then, I thought NO! He should be here with me! I'm so confused. I keep praying about what to do.

The Memphis Years

1972-1976

1972

JANUARY 1, 1972   Freezing! With wind chill, it has been -20! I'm gonna make changes in my life this year. Danny and I are still dating, but it's rough. He was calling nearly every night, but now it's once in a while. He says he wants to marry me and move to San Antonio. When he's home, I only see him on weekends. I love him and his kids. The divorce will be final soon. I'm lonely and don't know what to do.

I don't teach the toddlers in church now. I am the teacher of the young adults! What a switch! Everyone is so sweet. We have coffee and treats while we study God's Word. We get together on Sat. and Sun. nights to play games, watch movies and eat dinner. I love it. But, Danny won't go. I pray for God's answer to me.

JANUARY 2, 1972   The Imperials Quartet, a gospel group who recently toured with Elvis, came to church to perform. They are really great. It's no wonder Elvis had them as background singers. After the show, they answered questions. They stopped working with Elvis cuz they don't want to tour and be away from their families. Someone asked what Elvis was like to work with. They praised his talents but added, "All I can say is pray for Elvis." That stuck in my mind. I pray for him every night. Have to pray harder, I guess.

FEBRUARY 13, 1972   Juliette Prowse married.

FEBRUARY 23, 1972   Elvis and Priscilla separated! I can't believe it! How could she leave the sexiest, most loved man in the world?

MAY 14, 1972   Elvis is coming to the Chicago Stadium for a concert June 15! Tickets go on sale tomorrow! Have to go to Sears to get them.

MAY 15, 1972   I stood in line at Sears for 4 hours to get tickets. Everyone in line was buying Elvis tickets! I was afraid they would sell out. I prayed so hard that they wouldn't. I got tickets for me, Bon, Bon's sister Beth, and for Hazel. We're not sure how good the seats are, but we will be together. As I walked away, they announced that all the Elvis tickets were sold out! I thanked God I got tickets!

MAY 16, 1972   I found a lump in my breast. Made an apptointment with the doctor. He says the cyst is big. I really am scared. If it's cancer, my breast will be removed. I wrote Danny to tell him about it and about the Elvis concert.

JUNE 13, 1972   Haven't heard from Danny. I think he found someone else. Surgery is scheduled for June 28. Mom and Dad want to move to KY! I don't want to go. Can't afford to stay here alone. A horrible day. The only thing I have to look forward to is Elvis' concert in 3 days.

JUNE 16, 1972   Hazel was going to drive us to the concert, but she got sick. Her husband, Harold, drove instead and used her ticket. We left for Chicago at 6:00. We didn't know how the traffic would be, and we'd have to get a parking place. It was 7:40 when we got to our seats. I was afraid we'd be late. Our seats were on the top floors! Nothing blocked our view, but we were so far away. Guys sold binoculars; I bought a pair. The lights finally dimmed at 8:30. Jackie Cahane, a comedian, came on for about 15 minutes. He was pretty funny. Next, the Sweet Inspirations, a black girl gospel group sang for 30 minutes. They were Elvis' backup singers. Then a 30 minute intermission. We went to get a bite to eat and returned to our seats. Every seat in the place was filled. I saw Col. Parker and Joe Espisito by the stage. The lights were turned off. Music started playing. A spotlight appeared to the side of the stage. Elvis appeared! The room lit up like daylight from all the camera flash bulbs! My heart was jumping in my throat. He wore a skin tight, white jumpsuit. I don't know how he kept from ripping it. He was even more handsome than when I met him 10 years ago. He grabbed the mike and sang "That's All Right Momma." Other songs were: "Love Me Tender," "Treat Me Nice," "Hound Dog," "Lay Your Head Upon My Pillow," "Suspicious Minds," (he stooped down and sang "I hope this suit don't tear up, Baby") , " Little Sister," "I've Never Been to Spain," "All Shook Up," "Don't Be Cruel," "Can't Help Falling in Love With You," "American Trilogy," "Bridge Over Troubled Water," "Blue Suede Shoes," "Proud Mary," "Polk Salad Annie," and "You've Lost That Loving Feeling."

He joked around with the audience in between songs. Girls threw panties and bras up on the stage. Elvis walked to the Sweet Inspirations and asked if they belonged to them. Everyone laughed. He put the items on top of his head, wiped the sweat from his face, and threw them to the audience! A bunch of girls ran for them. A girl yelled "Elvis! Elvis! Elvis!" He looked at that directions and said, "I'll be up there in a minute, Honey." Screams and laughs from the audience. He joked about the Ed Sullivan shows, his shaky leg and his other shaky leg (shaking them and causing screams) and how he was filmed from the waist up so the TV audience couldn't see his lower body move. He has a great sense of humor and laughed about himself. The performance was 9:30-10:45. It was great! When he walked off stage, I couldn't believe he was done. He got a standing ovation. Everyone stood waiting for an encore. Finally, a voice announced: "Ladies and gentlemen, Elvis has left the building." I cried. I actually saw him perform in person! I love him so much!

I bought programs and pictures. We slowly made our way out of the theater. It seemed to take forever to get out of the parking lot. Once we got to the toll way, we were out of traffic. We talked about how great Elvis was, the show and the songs. Harold took lots of pictures with my camera. I pray they turn out all right. It was after midnight when we got home. I couldn't sleep. I just wanted to talk about the show. Bon and Beth fell asleep. I finally dozed off.

JUNE 28, 1972   I had surgery today. Thank God again that there is no cancer! I'll be able to go home in a few days. Will have to take it easy for a while.

JUNE 30, 1972   Mom and Dad put the house up for sale! I love to visit my family in KY, but I don't want to live there! It's way out in the country. About 20 miles from the nearest town! Everyone knows your business, plus they add to it. If you walk across the street, you're being watched and later rumors are you met with Joe Blow and had an affair! I'm not moving! I'll stay with Aunt Liz and continue working at Wards. Surgery, nothing from Danny, and now this! Why, dear God? Why?

JULY 1, 1972   Aunt Liz is moving to KY. She'll rent her house to Vi and I. Bon and I are moving to Memphis soon.

JULY 26, 1972   Priscilla filed for a legal separation from Elvis! Rumors are she is having an affair with her karate instructor. How could she? I can only imagine the heartache Elvis is going through. I pray for him every day. I'm so worried about him.

JULY 27, 1972   The Sunday school class is still going strong. About 30 of us for class and church. Some are dating others in the group. Vi and John are engaged. Hazel told me she heard from Danny. He's living with a woman; he plans to take his family to Texas. I can't say I'm surprised. I do love him, but I have to get on with my life. I'm glad I learned the truth about him before we married and I made a big mistake. I know the Lord wants me to go to Memphis. I'll find someone there. I know I will.

AUGUST 2, 1972   The alternator in my car broke down. Harold fixed it. I invited the Sunday school class over for a goodbye party. No one came! I started to cry. Vi and John asked me to go someplace with them. When we entered a strange house, a Doberman ran toward me. I turned to run out, but the owner grabbed him and took him away. I heard "Surprise!" The entire class was there! We had a great fellowship. I was elated and sad at the same time.

AUGUST 21, 1972   Elvis filed for a divorce on the 18th. I'm so heartbroken. They were such a loving couple made for each other.

AUGUST 26, 1972   Heard Elvis' new record "Burning Love." It sure is dirty! So many changes in his life. I pray I can talk to him and help get his mind straightened out. Maybe I can convince him to go back to Priscilla. If nothing else, for Lisa Marie's sake. How can poor Lisa understand that? I pray for the whole family every night.

SEPTEMBER 11, 1972   Bon and I packed all our belongings in our cars. Vi came to tell us goodbye. She told us, "Today is the first day of the rest of your life." I'll always remember that. We went to KY and stayed the night with Mom and Dad. They're staying in a little house until theirs is built. Mom wants me to move in with them. Aunt Liz says I won't stay in Memphis. Bon and I are determined that this is God's will for us.

SEPTEMBER 12, 1972   Left for Memphis at 11:30. It was a 4 1/2 hour drive. Got a room at a hotel on Hwy 51 near Graceland. We met a couple guys staying at the hotel. The four of us ate dinner together at a restaurant across the street. They asked to take us out later. Bon and I went to our room to settle in and relax for a while. The tub handle wouldn't turn. The guys came and fixed it for us. They left and said they would be back. Bon and I waited a couple hours, but they didn't return. We decided to go to bed. About 1:00 AM, I was awakened by bright lights shining in the hotel window. The guys knocked on the door and announced they were here to get us. We told them to go away. We were sleeping and had to get up early. They were upset but left. I was mad, too. They should have come back like they said they were.

SEPTEMBER 14, 1972   Bon and I found a furnished house for rent. Front entrance is a huge bedroom (Bon told me to take it). Bon's room is small. Upstairs has a kitchen, large living room and a bathroom with a shower. Closets are small, so a lot of clothes have to go in a chest or dresser. It's near downtown. No air or furnace. We use landlord's fan and there is a gas heater for winter. Rent is cheap. Glad we found something right away. We got unpacked and settled in. The landlords are young Christians with a baby. They're very nice and helpful. We looked for churches in the phone book.

SEPTEMBER 16, 1972   I got a job as a waitress at Shoney's restaurant near our place. I can only get part time, though, plus tips. The work will be hard, but I know I can do it. The hours will be 4-8 PM.

SEPTEMBER 17, 1972   Went to Graceland. Elvis is home! We met the guard, Harold Lloyd, Elvis' cousin. Vernon and Dee live in a home behind Graceland on the next street; it can be accessed from Elvis' gate in the back yard. Elvis' grandmother and aunt live with them. He takes care of them. That is so sweet. I also learned I was wrong about Elvis being alone! Linda Thompson, the former Miss Tennessee, is living with him! I couldn't believe it! How could he do that? He and Priscilla loved each other so much. And, Linda is younger than I am!

SEPTEMBER 26, 1972   Bon got a job as a bookkeeper at a dept. store, J B Hunter. I'll apply there tomorrow.

SEPTEMBER 27, 1972   Got a part time job at J B Hunters as a sales clerk. I'll work mornings, so I can still work at Shoneys. I will work 10 AM to-2 PM. It may turn into a full time job. So happy the Lord has blessed us with a place and jobs. I love this city. Everything is gonna be fine.

OCTOBER 8, 1972   We went to a church on Union and Parkway. It's big, but everyone is nice. We really would like a smaller place to worship. We're still searching. God will guide us to one we really feel at home in.

OCTOBER 13, 1972   Dating Bob, the manager of the restaurant at Hunters. He's nice, but he drinks too much. We have dinner and talk. A couple other guys have asked me out, too. The guys are so much nicer here!

OCTOBER 19, 1972   Mom and Dad are coming down to bring the rest of my clothes. I miss them. But, I love Memphis!

OCTOBER 20, 1972   Went to a Christian church near Whitehaven. It's a smaller building. They have 2 services to hold all the members. It is associated with the Christian College next door and the students attend their services. We met several teachers—young girls. So, we've made friends already. It's quite a drive from where we live, but we feel comfortable there. Everyone is so nice! We went to Graceland after church—Elvis is home! Stopped by Dee and Tony's to talk for a while. They're happy for us.

OCTOBER 22, 1972   Went to Graceland. Harold allowed me inside the gate and told me to go in the small guard shack. It's neat and clean and has a couch and chairs to sit on. A telephone sits by the window and is used to alert the guards that Elvis is coming down. I was shown the security cameras outside that are always on. I met a girl named April who lives by us. She's from Boston and is engaged to Harold's son. Everyone was nice to me, but April was the friendliest. She looks so much like Cher, a singer. She knows everyone and has a lot of friends. She's kinda loud and outspoken. I liked her right away. Elvis was expected to go to the movies, but he didn't. The only one to come down was one of Elvis' stepbrothers. He didn't stop.

OCTOBER 23, 1972   Went to work at Shoneys. They changed the schedule, so I didn't have to work. On the way to Graceland, my car started acting up. When I got to Graceland, Harold looked under the hood and said it looks like the water hose broke. He doesn't know how to repair cars, so I went home.

OCTOBER 24, 1972   Got up and took my car to a gas station to get it fixed. I went shopping and got a $40.00 human hair wig. It's the same color as my hair and long with waves and curls. Decided I can wear it instead of having to set and dry my hair all the time. Worked at Shoneys for a few hrs. Got a little bit in tips. Went home, washed my hair and uniform, dressed in jeans, put on my wig, and headed to Graceland. My car died again. Two nice guys stopped to help me. The repairman forgot to connect something! And, a piece was missing. One of the guys stayed with me and we talked about Elvis. He had seen him riding around town a few times. The other guy went to get the part. He returned, they both worked on in for a few min. The car started! I was so grateful! I offered to pay them for their effort, but they refused. They wouldn't even take money for the part! I was glad cuz I didn't have very much money with me. They both told me they hoped I'd get to see Elvis tonight. I said a prayer of thanks to God that the car was fixed. The guys were nice, they didn't take money, and they didn't try any hanky panky. Guys are so different here! Truly Southern gentlemen! There were no cars at Graceland. My heart sank. I told Harold about my car trouble. He told me Elvis had just left for the Memphian and the fans were invited to go along. I asked if he thought I'd get in. He shrugged his shoulders and said I could try, as Elvis was in a good mood. I drove as fast as I could and prayed all the way that I wouldn't get stopped speeding and that I could get in to see Elvis. The theater was dark (Elvis rents it after it's closed for the day). I drove around to the back. Elvis' Mark IV was there! I parked far away from it, but walked over to touch the door handle. My body trembled. I saw steps leading down to a door of the theater. I heard voices coming from the front, so I walked there. A couple guys stood there talking and smoking cigarettes. I approached them. I recognized Joe Esposito from his pictures in magazines. "Can I help you?" He asked snottily. I asked if Elvis was in there. He answered with an angry "Why?" I was getting angry and wanted to cry, but I controlled myself. I told him I heard Elvis was watching a movie and I might be able to get in. "Who told you?" I answered, "Harold. The guard at Graceland." He looked at me disgustedly, sighed, turned to the guy behind him and said, "Take her in, but keep her away from up front. Seat her on the right side, back row." I thanked him as I entered the theater.

The smell of fresh popcorn filled the air. I remembered I hadn't eaten dinner. I followed the guy to the room where the movie was showing. He took me to the 4th row from the back. He was nice and said, "You can sit here. Just don't go up front or bother Elvis." I thanked him and sat down. A horror movie was on and the screen was dark. It took a few minutes for my eyes to adjust. I was the only one seated in that area. Everyone else sat in the center aisles. I could hear Elvis talking and laughing. The guys laughed, too. I finally spotted where he was located. Center aisle. Midway back from the screen. No one sat in front of him. The movie was about witchcraft and boring. I was so tired. I could hardly keep my eyes open. My mind started wandering. I felt hungry. I was afraid to get up from my seat. I didn't know if the food was free or not. I remembered some peanut butter crackers in my purse. I reached in and retrieved them. I tried to open the package. The room was as quiet as church during the sermon. I could have heard a pin drop. I looked around to make sure no one was watching me.

Three men from the row where Elvis was stood and walked up the aisle toward me. Elvis was walking in front! He stopped, looked down and stared at me for a few seconds, and then went out to the lobby. He had only been 6" away from me! Charlie Hodge walked by me, smiled, and gently touched my head. I prayed he wouldn't rip the wig off! I managed to say hi and he left the room. My stomach was churning! I put the crackers back in my purse. I couldn't eat now!

A few minutes later, Elvis and the two guys came back and walked by me again. They returned to their seats. Not long after that, the movie ended. The lights came on. Elvis and his group stood and walked up the aisle toward me and out the door. Everyone stood, so I did, too. I grabbed all my stuff and walked to the lobby. The door to the men's room was directly in front of me. The door swung open and just missed hitting me! It was Elvis! He knew he almost hit me with the door. He stood staring at me. I wanted to throw my arms around him and hug and kiss him! My heart pounded! My brain was yelling "I love you!" I took a step toward him. I wanted to introduce myself and remind him of our first meeting. A man stepped in front of me. He had a woman he wanted Elvis to meet. I was disappointed, but I slowly walked to the middle of the room.

April and a few others from the guard shack were there. I joined them. They were surprised that I had gotten in. I asked if it was over. They said yes. It was obvious they didn't want to talk to me, so I walked to a pole and stood there.

I watched Elvis walk around the room. He went to a man who looked familiar (later I was told it was Mac Davis). I needed to use the ladies room. I saw a tall blonde and walked toward her to ask for directions. She saw me coming and turned her back to me. I figured what the heck and returned to my pole. (I learned later from April that it was Linda Thompson, Elvis' girlfriend).

Elvis continued to walk back and forth in front of me. I finally got up the nerve to say, "Hi, Elvis." He stopped, looked me in the face, nodded and winked at me. It seemed like an eternity before he walked away, but I know it was only a few seconds. I felt like he was reading my mind. He wore a crushed velvet blue or purple suit with a high collar, a white tie with blue or purple print. He had gained a little weight since I first met him. He had just returned from Vegas, so he was tanned. Everyone started leaving, so I left, too. I woke Bon up to tell her all about it. She said "Good." and went back to sleep.

OCTOBER 25, 1972   Off from JB's.   Still excited about last night. I dreamed about it. Everyone at Shoneys was happy and excited for me. Went to Graceland. Elvis had gone to the movies, but it was closed to the fans. When I told Harold I was allowed in the movies last night, everyone listened. They were all so much nicer to me. I was told to refer to the guard area as the Gate and the mansion as the House. Since I did not cause any trouble or noise and I got in the Memphian on my own, I would have access to enter the gates at all times. The group that hangs around there call themselves the "regulars." Harold gave me the private phone number to call the Gate. I can call any time and get information on what's happening! I am a regular at Elvis' home! WOW!

OCTOBER 26, 1972   Went to the Memphian after work. Elvis' Mach IV was there. All the regulars were standing outside talking. It was a closed party. I went home.

OCTOBER 27, 1972   Went to the Gate. Elvis drove down. He stopped, looked at me and waved. He drove away. He went to the Memphian, but no fans were invited. Someone said he got mad Monday night cuz people were talking to Mac Davis and ignoring him. I don't understand that, but they said all the shows would be closed from now on. I'm so grateful I was able to attend the last one, but I wondered if he was mad cuz I was there and he kept seeing me.

OCTOBER 28, 1972   Met another guard, Fred. He's shy and people don't like him. I think he's very nice. He's quiet and I have to start conversations. Elvis got home from the Memphian about 2:00 AM. He stopped and waved to me. I love that he knows I exist.

OCTOBER 31, 1972   It was a beautiful night. I wore my new hot pants suit to the Gate. Another closed show. No one goes to the Gate when Fred is on duty, so I was the only one there when Elvis came home driving his black Caddy. He stopped and waved to me then went to the House.

Harold is married, but he has a pregnant girlfriend named Martha. She got sick, so Harold took her to the House to lie down for a while. Harold went to get her.

I asked Fred if I could go up. He said sure. He walked me up the driveway. I had been to the House before, but never at night. A blue light shined and made it even more beautiful. Fred took me to the right of the House to the swimming pool. It's shaped like a kidney bean and it seems small to me. There were several lounge chairs surrounding it. We passed the pool, stepped down and there was a beautiful fountain with lights that change colors. It was so quiet. I felt at peace there. It's called Meditation Garden. There's a building with glass windows that have pictures (I couldn't see what the pictures were, as we were too far away). We went in the side entrance of the House. There's a hall with men's and ladies bathrooms with showers. The ladies room is the largest; it has a barber chair where Elvis sits to get his hair cut. I couldn't believe I was inside the House! I hoped Elvis would come, but he didn't. We walked back to the Gate, talking about the beauty of it all.

Charlie Hodge drove in the Gate, stopped and got out of the car. He entered the shack, went to Judy and playfully rubbed his hands on her arms to make her husband, Travis, jealous (he did). He looked me up and down and said, "Hi, Honey. How are you?" I smiled and said "Fine." Red West drove down and out of the driveway. I told Fred I believe God wants me to witness to Elvis. He thought it was a good thing. Elvis leaves tomorrow for a tour in California.

DECEMBER 6, 1972   Went to the Gate. Harold was teasing about taking me up to The House and having sex. I tried to make it into a joke, but then Charlie Hodge came down and made it clear he had the same intentions. I told them both no. Harold said if it was Elvis, I'd hop into bed. I told them both that I would sleep with no man, including Elvis, unless we were married. One of the regulars, Chris, went across the street with me to a gas station to use the washroom. She feels the same as I about sex. Her dad was a Pentecostal preacher. We talked religion and decided we're gonna try to witness to Elvis together!

DECEMBER 16, 1972   The Christmas decorations at Graceland are so beautiful! Blue lights are everywhere-- on the curb all the way to the House, on the House, trees and bushes. A life size manger scene is in the front yard. Harold walked me up so I could see it all up close. I didn't take my camera, so I didn't get a picture.

Only a few of the regulars are coming, since Elvis is gone. I go to keep Fred and Harold company. We talk a lot. Fred doesn't know much about the Presley's, but he shares the few things he's seen or heard about Elvis. Harold has a lot of stories. I told him I want to witness to Elvis. He said Elvis is a believer in God. He'd love to attend church, but he knows he would distract the service. He reads the Bible and prays a lot. He wants to change his career to be a gospel singer. He wants out of his contract with Col. Parker. Col. told him to go ahead, but if he hears Elvis singing anywhere—even in the shower—he'll sue Elvis for every penny he has. Harold agrees that Elvis is under a lot of stress. He told me Elvis has always had trouble sleeping—he's so hyper. He takes pills to sleep and to wake him up. Elvis doesn't like to sleep alone cuz he walks in his sleep and is worried he'll get hurt. He's also afraid of the dark! He wants a light on all night. Don't know if all that's true, but Harold is his cousin!

DECEMBER 24, 1972   Bon flew home for Christmas. I drove to KY to Mom and Dad's. They are in their new house. It is beautiful . They want me to move in with them. Mom said I can buy a horse, as there is plenty of room for it to roam. As much as I love horses and my parents, I don't want to live in KY.

Danny got in touch with Hazel and she asked Mom to have me call her. He wants me back! He went to IN to get his mom and kids and stuff, drove to San Antonio, went to the house and everything was gone! The woman stole everything! I don't feel sorry for him. He deserves what he got. I told Hazel I'm dating and having too much fun in Memphis. Besides, I see Elvis nearly every day, when he's home!

1973

JANUARY 1, 1973   I'm dating 3 guys from work—Herschel, Dennis, and Bob. They're nice. Nothing serious. April's roommate moved out and she's looking for someone to share the trailer with her. It has 3 bedrooms. Bon and I will go look at it. We're praying for an answer. Our landlords are nice, but the oil heater is not warm enough, and we have mice.

JANUARY 3, 1973   Went to see April's trailer. It's nice, but not enough closet space. Not sure what to do. I like the fact that it's across the street from Elvis.

JANUARY 8, 1973   Elvis' birthday. This is the first year I haven't sent a card. We got snow and ice! So many accidents. Rare for this area. People don't know how to drive in this. They don't use salt on the roads just sand. Unbelievable!

JANUARY 17, 1973   Bob wants to get married! I'm having too much fun to marry now. I want to be friends with all the guys.

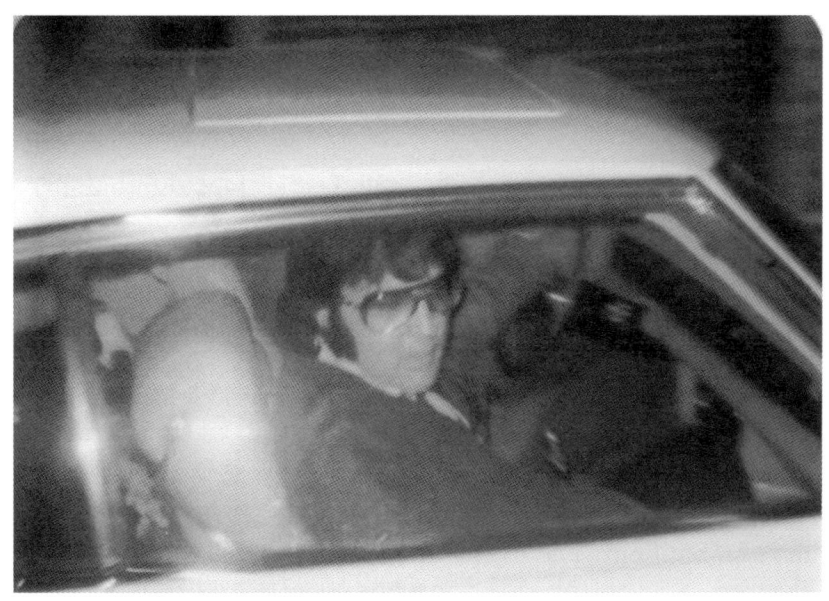

JANUARY 21, 1973   Mom's birthday. Seems strange not to be with her. JB Hunters is doing inventory. I'll have a lot of overtime. Don't like the idea, but I can use the extra cash. I got a raise, too, and I'll be working full time.

January 22, 1973   Bob is insisting on marrying me! I keep praying. I like him, but I'm not ready for marriage right NOW. At work I saw a woman in the baby dept. Didn't have my glasses on, and she was far away. That baby was ugly! I went to her to help and learned the baby was a monkey! She works at the Memphis zoo and is raising the baby at home! He's so sweet. She laughed when I told her the ugly baby thing! President Lyndon Johnson died.

JANUARY 29, 1973   Harold called me. Elvis will be home the first of April.

FEBRUARY 1, 1973   Lisa Marie's birthday. Wonder if Elvis will be able to see her.

FEBRUARY 5, 1973   Bob and I had it out tonight! All he wants to do is go to bars and get drunk. Since he has been going to church with me, I thought he would change. Tonight he told me my God is a hoax. That was it! I drove him home. He tried to makeup, but when I looked in his face, I could see the devil. It scared me. I made him get out of my car and I left. No one talks about my Lord like that! I told him it's over. I'll never talk to him again!

FEBRUARY 11, 1973   Mom and Dad came to bring my stuff. They looked at the house and said they were moving us to a better place. While I was at work, Mom and Dad moved our stuff to another place! It's in a much better neighborhood. The rent is only a few dollars higher than we were paying. 4 apt. building. Two bedrooms, small bath and kitchen, a huge living room, and a porch to sit on. We love it! Couldn't believe it all happened so fast. Dad paid the first month's rent and told us not to worry about it. He and Mom want us to be safe.

FEBRUARY 25, 1973   Got my Tenn. driver's license! I studied for a written test, but I only had to take the eye test. Tenn. only accepts certain states licenses. Some of the girls from church had to have written and driving tests. Glad that's over! Tenn. doesn't charge State tax on license plates. Everyone pays $12.50—even Elvis on his expensive cars! Everyone who lives or works in Memphis must buy a Memphis City sticker for $10.00. No State tax on payroll! I love this place! Everything is cheap.

FEBRUARY 29, 1973   Harold asked me to guard the place while he went to get something to eat! Wow! If Elvis was home, it wouldn't have happened. I was scared someone would come, but no one did. I can't believe I'm trusted that much! I feel so important! Part of Elvis' life!

MARCH 1, 1973   Elvis and Pris' divorce is final. Pictures in Memphis Commercial Appeal show them walking out of the court house and kissing before parting. I can't believe he went through with it. I don't know what he sees in Linda. He has to pay support and alimony. Graceland is still his. It would break his heart to lose it. I feel sorry for Lisa Marie. They have joint custody. Pris agreed to let him have her according to his schedule. Glad that worked out. Still wish they'd get back together.

MARCH 8, 1973   Called Fred. Elvis' Mach IV has been going in and out but he's not in the car. They think he's in town hiding out some place.

MARCH 10, 1973   Tornado warnings. Didn't go to the Gate. Vernon told Vester to be expecting Elvis home soon.

MARCH 11, 1973   Mom and Dad called. They are moving back to Ind. Dad's boss called him and convinced him to move back as there is a lot of work. I knew they wouldn't be happy in KY. I dread having to go so far to visit. I'm not leaving Memphis. Called Harold. Elvis is still not home.

MARCH 12, 1973   Went to children's hospital to sit with a baby from church who has a tumor. She can't be alone and the parents don't have money to pay for private help. The congregation is volunteering to sit with her while the parents work. Took forever to find the place, but I did. Elvis is not home.

March 16, 1973   My 25th birthday. Lots of people at work got me gifts. Herschel drew a picture of Jesus and the little children. It's pretty. He's very nice but a momma's boy. He doesn't think marriage is important. I only think of him as a friend.

MARCH 20, 1973   Elvis' grandfather, Jesse Presley, died. Vernon and Vester went to Louisville for the funeral. Vester told Harold Elvis is still in Vegas. He has pneumonia! He's not able to perform. The Imperials and Stamps Quartet are filling in for Elvis. Not sure when he'll be home.

MARCH 22, 1973   I am full time at JB Hunter! I quit Shoneys!

APRIL 9, 1973   Talked to Harold. Elvis bought a $22,000.00 motorcycle and had it delivered to Graceland. Can't believe he spent that much money for it!

MAY 13, 1973   Elvis is still touring. Went to the Gate. Vester was on duty. When Harold came, we all talked for a long while. I had to use the ladies room. Vester took April and me up to the House to use the bathroom! I can't believe I'm so trusted! I have access to the grounds, the Gate is automatically opened for me, and I have all the telephone numbers! Vernon and Dee separated.

MAY 15, 1973   Vernon and Dee are getting divorced. Not trying to make up.

May 17, 1973   Watergate trial started.

May 18, 1973   Elvis' tour in Lake Tahoe ends Sunday. He'll probably come home.

May 19, 1973   Harold called. Elvis' tour was cancelled. He has tonsillitis. He has a concert scheduled in Nashville in June.

May 20, 1973   Harold called. Elvis is home. He was out on the grounds walking with Vernon. Nancy and Ramonda are here from St. Louis. Went to see them. We sat and talked about Vegas and Elvis' other concerts. We all exchange pictures of Elvis, as well as stories. One big, happy family. Elvis didn't go out this evening.

MAY 21, 1973   I worked 10-6. Got to the Gate at 10:30. Elvis didn't go out. Charlie Hodge drove in the Gate, stopped and yelled, "Hi, Harold! Hi, Sandy!" I was so surprised. He had seen me a couple times, but we'd never been introduced. We talked for a while and I asked how he knew my name. He said, "We know more about you people at the Gate than you think we do." He told details of happenings he was aware of. Spooky. Martha moved back to Ohio with the baby. Harold can't afford to take care of them. He keeps hinting about me going to the House with him. I won't get in the same predicament Martha did. Elvis bought a Bear Cat Stutz car. Nice looking but weird. It's hand-made and very expensive!

May 23, 1973   Elvis didn't go out. Charlie came down to talk. I had my pic taken with him. He's really nice. I'd like to get to know him better. One girl from Conn. said she wants to date Charlie to meet Elvis. I told her I couldn't use anyone like that. Went to Krystals for burgers, then back to the Gate. Charlie drove out just as I was leaving. We waved.

MAY 24, 1973   Elvis went out about 8:00. I was at work and missed seeing him. He and Linda broke up, but she is back with him tonight. Don't know what happened. No one does.

MAY 25, 1973   Elvis and Charlie didn't go out. Kenny Hicks, a new bodyguard for Elvis, came down to the Gate to talk to us. He's a preacher's son and a nephew to one of the Stamps Quartet. He asked me to go out with him. We'll get together soon.

MAY 26, 1973   Pris modeled for some pictures in a bathing suit. Word is Elvis is furious about it. She's pretty and has a nice shape, but the pictures were provocative.

MAY 27, 1973   Dr. Nick went up to the House. He didn't stay long. Hope Elvis isn't still sick. Kenny took April to breakfast earlier. When he came down this evening, he kept staring at me.

MAY 28, 1973   Got to the gate about 11:00. Elvis' stepbrother, David, and Kenny were there. Harold, Carol and I talked about the Bible. Dr. Nick's car literally flew up the driveway. We wondered what was wrong. He came down shortly, so we figured everything was OK.

MAY 29, 1973   Met a real nice guy named Tom at the Gate. We talked about the Bible. Elvis' stepbrother, Ricky, and Kenny came down on golf carts. Kenny asked me to go for a ride. I said sure and climbed on. He turned the headlights off. He started racing with Ricky. What a ride! We were riding in the grass between all the trees. I held on for dear life. I thought I was gonna get killed! We drove around the House several times before going back to the Gate. We talked a bit before Kenny and Ricky left to go to the House. I'll never forget that ride!

MAY 30, 1973   Elvis didn't go out, but Charlie and Vernon went out separately. We're all scared Elvis must really be sick.

MAY 31, 1973   Elvis was out riding the golf cart for a couple hours in the afternoon. He didn't go out at night. Vernon and Charlie went out separately.

JUNE 3, 1973   Got to the Gate about 9:30. Elvis came down in his new Stutz. I lined my camera to take a pic of him. He stopped right in front of me so I could take one! It's the first one I've taken of him! He drove around town and returned home.

    Kenny came down in his car and asked me to get in to go with him to Vapors for a drink. He drove to the hotel where he was staying. Said he had to get something and told me to come in for a minute. We talked for a few minutes about Elvis. I asked him to go to church with me. Said he was too busy to go and that Elvis needed him to be close by. He stood and changed his jacket. He was wearing a holster gun! He saw it scared me, so he quickly explained that Elvis has been getting a lot of death threats. All the guys wear guns to protect Elvis! He warned me not to tell anyone. I promised I wouldn't. We talked for a long while. He hinted that he would take me to the House and introduce me to Elvis if I slept with him. I told him no. I am a Christian and he should know better because his father is a preacher. He got mad and took me back to the Gate. I got out of the car. Everyone saw I was angry. Kenny tried to talk to April and Chris, but they ignored him. They sensed something was wrong. He drove up to the House alone. I pray he doesn't start any rumors about me. I thank God for protecting me.

JUNE 4, 1973   Elvis had rented the fairgrounds a couple nights ago. April and I decided to check it out. No one was there. Went to the Crosstown Theater. Elvis' Stutz was there. The show was closed. So many people were there. April and I were tired, so we left and went home.

JUNE 5, 1973   Elvis rented the Memphian. Show was closed. Elvis is on a white car kick. He bought new cars for all the guys, Linda, and Dr. Nick. Linda didn't like hers, so she returned it and traded it in for a blue one! I told everyone I wouldn't care what color it was! I would have been grateful to receive a free car from anyone—especially Elvis!

While Elvis was buying the cars, a woman was looking in the window at him (it was after hours and the store was closed). Elvis walked out to her and asked if she wanted a new car. She said yes. He told her to pick out the one she wanted—he bought it for her!

JUNE 7, 1973 Kenny came to the Gate. He sat down by me and talked about God. He's not mad any more. Thank God!

JUNE 12-16, 1973   Drove to KY to visit Mom and Dad and the family. Shared my experiences with Elvis. Mom and Dad don't understand why I won't move back to Ind. Memphis is home now. Got back to Memphis late.

JUNE 17, 1973   Elvis had not gone out all the time I was in KY. He came down about 11:30, stopped the car and waved to me. I got another good pic of him. Kenny took April and me to the House for a few minutes. He gave me the telephone numbers to the House and the office.

JUNE 18, 1973   Elvis sneaked out the back way, so I didn't see him. I decided not to follow him. He was stopped by a traffic accident. He signed autographs for about 10 min.

JUNE 19, 1973   I just missed Elvis as he left for the airport. Some girls got close enough to the plane to get pics. They gave me some. Harold knew I was disappointed, so he took me up to the House by the pool. I told him I will have a white car one day and drive up here. He laughed and said OK.

JUNE 21, 1973   Bon has been having problems with her periods. The doctor told her she has a cyst on her ovary and needs it removed. She made an appointment with my surgeon, Dr. Thomas, in Ind. She left today. I'm praying so hard for her.

JUNE 24, 1973   Bon had surgery. One ovary had to be removed. She can still bear children, though. No cancer! Thank God! She'll be in Ind. about 6 weeks.

JUNE 26, 1973   Midge and J.D. from church asked if a lady named Sandy Young can stay with me while Bon is away. She's from Ark. She moved here to work. She's an alcoholic and has been in a hospital recovering. She'll be getting aid from the government soon that will pay for her housing. I agreed to let her stay with me for a while.

JUNE 30, 1973   Mom called to tell me she and Dad visited Bon. She's doing OK.

JULY 1, 1973   I picked Sandy up for church. She was baptized! Thank God! We packed her stuff and moved it to my place. She'll stay in Bon's room until she gets her own place or Bon gets back.

JULY 2, 1973   Took Sandy to the Gate. She was so excited to be allowed on the grounds. She's nice. I'm glad to have company with me.

July 3, 1973   Took Sandy shopping. On the way home, I was stopped at a red light. A girl ran into the back end of my car! There is a lot of damage to my car, but it's drivable. At the policeman's request, Sandy and I went to the hospital. We are both in pain, but nothing is broken. Went to the Gate. Elvis went out but didn't stop for pix. Sandy was thrilled to see him. Charlie drove down, stopped and talked to me for a minute then left.

JULY 4, 1973   Bon called. She's leaving the hospital tomorrow. She's homesick for Memphis! She feels good. Elvis went out and stopped for pix. Charlie stopped and talked a second but didn't get out of the car. I'm still so sore from the accident.

JULY 5, 1973   Still sore, but not like yesterday. Elvis drove down and was beeping his horn. He was in a good mood and waved, but he didn't stop. Charlie came down, got out and talked and joked with us for over an hour. He said they were going to the Memphian, but the show was closed. I didn't like Charlie at first, but I think I have a crush on him now.

JULY 7, 1973   Tony's birthday. Dee called. Little Sandy is getting married! Elvis didn't go out. Charlie came and talked for a long time.

JULY 8, 1973   April and I followed Elvis to the Memphian. We went to the door and knocked. Someone opened it, recognized us, and told us to come in. A big crowd came out of nowhere and ran to us. The door closed! We were so close to being inside! April and I were furious! We walked past the crowd and left.

JULY 9, 1973   Got an estimate for damage to my car. $82.00! Little Sandy called—she's getting married in Sept. Elvis went to the Memphian. Got some good pics of him. Hope they turn out.

July 11, 1973   Got a very nice pic of Elvis!

JULY 18, 1973   Insurance will pay for my car to be fixed. Bon is home! I'm so glad! I missed her. Sandy is sleeping in the living room on the couch.

JULY 20, 1973   Elvis rode in the back seat of the car, so I couldn't see him.

JULY 21, 1973   I was too tired to go to the Gate. Tom called to tell me Chris and another girl got past the guard and went to the House! They saw Lisa Marie and were talking to her. Elvis was mad! He called the guard and had him escort the girls out. Everyone had to leave. We don't know if anyone will ever be allowed in again.

JULY 22, 1973   The Gate was open, but no one went in. We were afraid Elvis was still mad. Someone drove Elvis down. He and Lisa Marie were in the back seat.

JULY 23, 1973   Pris is giving interviews with magazines about her life with Elvis. We hear he is very angry. Sandy still hasn't gotten her money from the state.

JULY 26, 1973   Bon went to the Gate with me. It's the first time she saw Elvis. She thinks it's OK, but she has a crush on one of the guys of the Imperials. She wants Sandy to move. Sandy is nice, but she relies on us for everything like a child. It feels strange. I'll talk to Midge and J D.

JULY 27, 1973   Went to the Gate. Lisa rode down by herself on a golf cart. She's a doll. She looks so much like her dad. She didn't say much, answered a few questions about how she is, etc. She drove away.

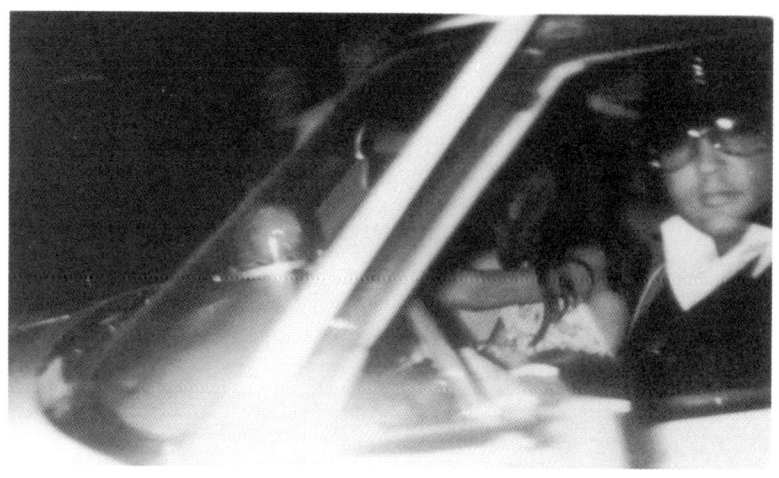

JULY 29, 1973   Elvis left. I just missed seeing him.

AUGUST 7, 1973   Went to South Central Bell Telephone Company to apply for a job. A lot of people were there. We went to a room to take timed tests. I didn't have any problems with any of the questions. We were asked to go to the waiting room. People were called in one by one to another room. They were only in for less than a minute and then came out and left. I was one of a few people waiting. Finally, I was called in. I passed the tests! They interviewed me and told me they would be in touch with me within the next couple months. Went to Sears for an eye exam. I need new glasses.

AUGUST 9, 1973   I got my glasses. They're a new kind that turn dark in the sunshine and replace wearing sunglasses. Cool. Went to the gospel show downtown. So many great groups. Uplifting experience. Glad I went. Elvis usually goes to at least one show, but he's not home.

AUGUST 11, 1973   My car is leaking oil and it stalls. Mr. Holly, the head of Security at work, sold me a big, old Chevy. It's in good condition, except the gas gauge doesn't work.

AUGUST 15, 1973   The telephone company called—I got the

job! I'll be an operator in a new facility. I'll work split shifts. My car stalls. Mr. Holly told me to put more than a gallon of gas in it. Cost $1.80! I can't afford that!

AUGUST 24, 1973   My last day to work at J B Hunter. They got me a charm bracelet with a telephone on it. It's so cute. I'll miss them all, but I'll make a lot more money with Ma Bell. Air conditioning on my car broke. I'll see if Dad can fix it tomorrow.

AUGUST 25, 1973   Left early for Mom's. She and Dad looked at my car, said "Come on. We're going shopping in Princeton." They bought me a 1973 Buick Opel! It's small, white, and beautiful! I love it! I've never owned a brand new car! I'll pay Mom and Dad monthly til it's paid for. Bon is gonna be surprised!

AUGUST 26, 1973   I got sunburned driving back to Memphis. I parked the car in front of our apartment building and went upstairs. Bon and Sandy were glad I made it OK. I told them something bad happened to my car and to look at it. They screamed when they saw my car. We went for a ride. Later, I went to the Gate and blew my horn. Harold came out. He was surprised! He said I scared him—he thought Elvis came home early! I told him to get in and I'd drive him to the House. He shook his head. I reminded him of what he told me about having a brand new, white car. He said OK and got in. He laughed all the way up and down the driveway. He never believed this would happen any more than I did. I drove slowly and looked all around. I love Graceland.

AUGUST 27, 1973   I reported to work at 8:00. I'll be in training for 3 weeks. I'll listen to tapes, use a computer that activates it (it's called TSPS). It's not like the ones on TV or movies. It's neat. I'll work 7-4:30 PM til I'm trained, and then shifts. The earliest I will have to work is 7:00 and they close at 11:00 PM. I'll get at least $100.00 a week, unless I work overtime, holidays, splits, or Sundays—I'll get more! It's boring but scary now. I'm gonna like it.

AUGUST 28, 1973   I've met so many friends at the Gate from all over the world. Aileen from Ireland and Pauline from England come to stay the summer to see Elvis in Vegas. Nancy, Sue, and Ramanda from St. Louis. Plus, all those who live here. Tom Kirby is so nice that he lets people stay with him in his apt. Lots of guys go to the Gate to meet girls. We all love and respect Elvis. We trade pics of him and stories of things that have happened. No one wants to make trouble—we just want to get a glimpse of him.

After my Memphian meeting, I said I would be satisfied with that. I was told NO! The more you see him, the more you want to see him! He's addictive like a drug. I thought they were nuts, but they're right. He's so handsome and exciting—just watching him walk or ride by is a thrill! He's so friendly and gracious. He loves his fans, as much as we love him!

We noticed the security cameras were on and facing the Gate. Someone had a radio on. I said "Let's dance and entertain them!" We did. A few minutes later, the phone rang. Harold answered it and came out laughing. Elvis and the guys were watching us! We had stopped for a minute, and they told us to dance some more! We laughed and danced. We hoped they would come down and get us, but they didn't. It was funny entertaining Elvis—instead of him being the show!

AUGUST 29, 1973   There was a big crowd at the Gate—mostly all my friends and me. Elvis went out, and we followed him. I caught up to him and got behind him. He sped up and I did, too. I passed him, and he passed me. I decided to get to the Memphian first, so I floored it. A few minutes later, I saw a police light and heard a siren. I pulled over. It was Elvis! He beeped, waved and went ahead. I went after him again. Suddenly, a real police car was behind me! I pulled over, knowing I'd get a ticket. The cop went on by and chased after Elvis and his gang! He pulled two of the cars over but let me go on! I sighed for relief. I vowed to never do that again! Elvis didn't get stopped, and he beat us to the Memphian.

SEPTEMBER 3, 1973   The elders from church found a place for Sandy. I pray she won't get back with the wrong crowd and start drinking again. I love her, but it's too crowded in our apartment. Sandy has made it clear she doesn't want to leave us, but she agreed to go. We will pick her up and take her to church. She won't be abandoned.

SEPTEMBER 10, 1973   Called Harold. They don't know when Elvis will be home, but there is a lot of remodeling being done at the House.

SEPTEMBER 12, 1973   Still in training at work. I'm dealing with real customers now. The super is sitting with me and listening in and helping when I need it. I still get nervous, but I'm told I'm doing great. Bon got a raise at her job! Maybe we can afford to move to a place closer to church.

SEPTEMBER 29, 1973   Called Harold. Elvis is still not home. Someone saw Kenny at the Gospel show with his dad. Elvis got mad at

Kenny and fired him and some others. We don't know what's going on. Tom and I have been going to movies together. He's a real good friend.

OCTOBER 1, 1973   Steve talked to Red West and shared some new with us. Kenny and Lamar were fired. James was caught stealing rings and other items from Elvis. Elvis was so mad that he hit a wall to avoid striking James. Elvis' hand is broken. All tours have been cancelled until the end of the year.

OCTOBER 5, 1973   Called the Gate. Linda went to the House and came back down and left. Elvis isn't home. Sandy started nurses' training. She still goes to church with us. Happy she's getting her life together.

OCTOBER 8, 1973   Harold said Elvis will be home Wed. I'm so glad. I miss him and Charlie so much.

OCTOBER 10, 1973   Elvis and Pris' divorce is final. Vice President Agnew resigned because of the Watergate trial. That's about all that's on the news. Linda keeps going to the House and leaving. Don't know what is happening.

OCTOBER 12, 1973   Elvis came home at 4:00 this morning. He went out in the black Stutz.

OCTOBER 15, 1973   I had a strange dream last night about Elvis. He was very sick. He was soaking wet with sweat and said he was freezing. His whole body was shivering. He called out my name. I was startled and woke up crying and trembling. It was 1:00 AM. I couldn't go back to sleep. Later, as I got ready for work, I heard on the radio that Elvis was admitted to Baptist Memorial Hospital with pneumonia at 1:00 this morning! The same time I dreamed it! I'm afraid Elvis might die cuz he has been sick for so long. Charlie isn't here. Some say he quit his job, some say he's visiting his parents. I'm so worried about Elvis and Charlie. Something is wrong.

OCTOBER 16, 1973   Elvis has recurring pneumonia. Vester said Elvis is doing a little better and can't wait to go home. April called and asked me to take her to the humane society. Her dog, Luv, is missing. He showed up at her place later.

OCTOBER 17, 1973   Liz called me. She talked to Vernon today. He's really worried about Elvis. Elvis is not doing any better, and they're running all kinds of tests on him. Liz asked if she could give him a gift for Elvis. Vernon said he would give the gift to Elvis personally. She's getting a friend to paint a picture. I'll write a letter and we'll attach it to the gift. Went to the Gate. Vernon came down, but he didn't stop. I'm disappointed. I wanted to talk to him.

OCTOBER 18, 1973   I spent most of last night writing my letter to Elvis. I pray he will read it and be touched by my witnessing to him. I pleaded with him to turn to God for help. I invited him to church. I told him my preacher would be happy to listen to him and help in any way possible. I am so worried about him.

OCTOBER 19, 1973   Liz didn't call. She is sick. I'm gonna tell her to forget the picture. I'll try to give the letter to Vernon. Charlie still hasn't come here.

OCTOBER 20, 1973   Went to church and to the Gate to meet Liz. She was late. We went to Vernon's house. He wasn't home. The guard there was real snotty to us. I told him we had a gift for Elvis and that Vernon agreed to give it to him. He just said, "He's not home." He closed the door. We went back to the Gate. Fred said Vernon was up at the House. He took the painting and my letter up for us. Fred returned and said Vernon told him Elvis is a little better, but they'll run more tests on Tuesday.

OCTOBER 21, 1973   Harold has a horrible cold. I told him if he's not better tomorrow to stay home and I'll guard the House. We'll see. Ricky Stanley went to the House to get Elvis something to eat—he doesn't like the hospital food.

OCTOBER 22, 1973   Ricky got food from the House again. I pray that's a sign Elvis is getting better, and I pray he got my letter.

OCTOBER 23, 2973   Reports say Elvis is teasing the nurses, so he must be getting better. Lots of people want President Nixon impeached. Cease fire in Israel.

OCTOBER 24, 1973   Elvis will be hospitalized for at least two more weeks. April wants all of us to rent a billboard near Graceland and put a message to Elvis to get well. I think it's a great idea. She's gonna check into it.

OCTOBER 27, 1973   April called to tell me Charlie is back! He went to the hospital to see Elvis. I'm so glad he's back! I love him!

OCTOBER 29, 1973   There were a lot of strangers at the Gate. Charlie went out to see Elvis. As he drove down, he looked at everyone kinda funny. When he saw, me, he smiled and waved and drove off.

NOVEMBER 1, 1973   Elvis is home. No one knows for sure how he is or what is really wrong. No news from the House.

NOVEMBER 5, 1973   Dad's birthday. Tom called to tell me Elvis went out for about 4 hours Saturday night.

NOVEMBER 6, 1973   Chris, Tom, and I were discussing religion at the Gate when Charlie came down. He listened for a while and then left. I keep praying I can talk to him and eventually to Elvis about God and our church.

NOVEMBER 7, 1973   Chris, Otis, Tom, and I discussed religion again tonight. I prayed that I could get a chance to talk to Charlie. As I finished, Charlie drove down from the House. We asked him to come in. He shook his head and drove away. I prayed to myself that God would give me the opportunity to talk to him. Twenty minutes later, Charlie returned. He parked his car and joined us in the guard shack. We were discussing witchcraft and psychics. Liz asked him if he had seen the painting she and I gave to Elvis; he hadn't. She asked what he and Elvis believe in religiously. He said Elvis believes in the religion of the mind. Charlie believes in metaphysics. Charlie stood, said he had to leave, and walked outside. Liz told me to go after him. I was scared, but she convinced me.

I prayed to say the right words. We sat in his car and began talking. I told him I have been praying for him and Elvis. I said that Imperials plea to pray for Elvis is what convinced me to move to Memphis—to witness to Elvis. He seemed shocked. We shared our religious beliefs openly and truthfully--and he told me Elvis' as well. We all accept God as the Supreme Ruler and Creator of the world and Jesus as His Son sent as the sacrifice for our sins. We discussed the Bible, quoted scriptures, talked about sex before marriage, marriage, (he loves a 19 year old preacher's daughter IF he marries, she will be the one)—about everything! My heart broke about the girl, but I tried to not let it show.

I told him of my dream about Elvis being ill and calling out to me and learning he was hospitalized at the exact time I dreamed it. He looked deep in thought then said it could be possible that Elvis and I have a spiritual connection, since I pray so earnestly for him. He said he believes it is true! I do also! I asked what he thought I should do. He held my hand, looked into my eyes, and said, "Continue praying for Elvis and me. We both need your prayers desperately. Elvis is physically and emotionally depressed and ill. Please continue your prayers. I will tell Elvis about you and how you are praying for us both. He will be very grateful."

I promised I would continue my prayers. I asked if he thought he Elvis and I could get together to discuss these things. He shook his head, looked me square in the eyes and said, "No. You're too nice of a girl to be up at the House." I felt insulted and praised at the same time. We decided it was late, and he needed to go up to bed. He kissed my cheek. We said goodnight. I got out of the car. As he drove off, Charlie yelled, "Don't forget to pray for us!" I went into the shack. Liz wanted to know all we talked about. I shared some of it, especially that Charlie would tell Elvis about me praying for him.

NOVEMBER 8, 1973   Liz called me. She talked to Charlie this afternoon. She told him what a nice girl I am. A lot of fun, a good dancer, and a Christian. She told Charlie I'm in love with him and asked why he didn't invite me to the House or on a date. He told her I was very nice, he likes me, but I'm too "straight" for him. Liz was mad. She told him, "Yes. She is too straight and too nice for any of you guys up on the hill—including Elvis!" I was mad at her, but I realized later that she was defending me. I was perfectly happy just being with Charlie. I never intended for him to learn my feelings for him. I'm afraid Charlie will never talk to me again.

NOVEMBER 9, 1973   Elvis went to Palm Springs and took Charlie with him. I had hoped to talk to him again. For some reason, Linda didn't go with Elvis. She's up at the House.

NOVEMBER 11, 1973   Harold called and said Linda left the House.

November 12, 1973   Threats were made on Lisa's life. The Gate is closed and extra security is around. Only the regulars are allowed inside. We don't know if Lisa is home or with Elvis.

NOVEMBER 13, 1973   Pauline called me from England to find out about the threats against Lisa. I guess the whole world knows about it.

NOVEMBER 14, 1973   Elvis' Hawaiian Special was on TV. Liz invited me for dinner at her home with her family (she has 6 kids). It was so exciting! He was wonderful! The audience loved him. Just looking at him, no one would have guessed he had been ill. I don't know why the show wasn't broadcast in the States the same time as the rest of the world saw it. He broke a world record—no one has been seen on satellite before! I'm proud of him.

NOVEMBER 15, 1973   Elvis sneaked back home.

NOVEMBER 25, 1973   Elvis drove down and stopped and waved to me. His window was rolled down, so I said hi. He smiled and said "Hi, Honey." I took a pic and he left.

November 27, 1973   Elvis was out. Harold had me get my car and we drove up to the House. He took me around the House, pointing out the bedroom, etc.

NOVEMBER 30, 1973   Elvis came out. Linda's parents drove up to the House. A few minutes later, Elvis returned and flew up the driveway. Linda's parents left in a hurry. Charlie entered the Gate. Said he couldn't talk and had to get to the House. Something was wrong. I stayed until 3:00 AM. No one came down. I left.

DECEMBER 1, 1973   Elvis came down and stopped for me to take a pic, but my camera didn't work. I was sick. He was so close to me.

DECEMBER 2, 1973   Charlie moved out of the House! He's staying in a motel down the street. Shirley C. and her mom and I went to talk to him. We all sensed something was wrong, but didn't know what. Charlie said he can't stand the pressure at the House any more. Vernon and Elvis are arguing about Linda spending too much money. Elvis says it's HIS money and he can spend it any way he wants. Charlie admitted that he and none of the guys like Linda. They feel she's using him. Elvis says no. Charlie's blood pressure is too high, so he moved out until he can get himself back to normal.

DECEMBER 3, 1973   We had planned a Christmas party at the Gate. Charlie called and said he couldn't come. Elvis was cutting an album at Stax Studios.

DECEMBER 4, 1973   Hardly no one was at the Gate. Chris and Otis said Elvis just left for Palm Springs. I stayed to talk to Harold. A few hours later, Elvis drove up. He stopped, smiled, and waved to me—I was the only one there!

DECEMBER 7, 1973   Tony came to look for a job. He wants to see if he can be a guard for Elvis. He went to the Gate with me. It would be nice to have my brother working for Elvis! Charlie moved back to the House. Elvis went to the Memphian. When he returned, he stopped and waved to me. I got a nice pic. Charlie was behind him. He stopped and got out of the car. I introduced him to Tony. They shook hands. I'm glad Charlie is still talking to me!

DECEMBER 13, 1973   I spotted Elvis' car just as I pulled off the expressway on my way to the Gate. I turned around and followed him. He got off the expressway and went downtown. It was late and dark. He pulled onto a back road, sped up, and I lost him. I was scared. I had never been there before. I made sure my doors were locked and prayed to find my way home. I looked up and saw an airplane that was headed for the airport. I knew which direction to head! I thanked God, followed the plane back toward Whitehaven. I finally got home. Thank God!

DECEMBER 14, 1973   Went to the Gate. Found out where Elvis went last night. A poor black family lost everything they owned in a house fire. Elvis had it investigated to learn where the family is now. He and the group went there personally and gave them a decorated tree, food, presents, everything they needed! The woman was crying on the news about how grateful she was, and how scared she was when she opened the door and saw Elvis standing there! He is such a wonderful man! April and I followed Elvis to Stax Studio. We sat outside and listened to the music. We could hear Elvis singing! So exciting!

DECEMBER 17, 1973   President Nixon passed a law to keep us on Savings time to save energy. Gas is getting low in supply.

DECEMBER 19, 1973   Elvis hasn't gone out the past several days.

He must be finished recording. Rumors are that he and Linda may marry Christmas day or his birthday.

DECEMBER 20, 1973   Took Bon to the train station. She's going to Ind. for Christmas. Singer Bobby Darrin died while having heart surgery. He was only 37.

DECEMBER 22, 1973   Mom and Dad came. So good to see them. I miss them so much. They asked how I would feel if they adopted a baby. They both have kids from previous marriages, but Mom could not bear children after Tony. A second cousin of mine is unmarried and pregnant. Her parents won't let her keep the baby. She asked Mom and Dad to adopt the baby. She knows the baby will be well taken care of. I said yes! I'm so excited! I always wanted a baby sister! Mom quickly added it could be another brother! Tony and my 3 stepbrothers are enough. I want a little sister!

DECEMBER 25, 1973   No snow and it's very warm. Doesn't seem like Christmas. We opened our gifts. Mom and Dad brought my gift from Bon's mom. She made me a beautiful, floor length, gold satin backless dress. Mom made a gorgeous black velvet cape for me to wear with it. They both fit me so well! Mom and Dad left for KY. They will tell my cousin they will adopt the baby and go to Ind. tomorrow. They asked me to move back home. Sometimes I want to, but I love Memphis and Elvis too much to leave. I'm dating more guys than I ever did in Ind.!

DECEMBER 30, 1973   Elvis and Linda didn't marry. I am so glad. Now, we'll wait and see about a birthday wedding. Went to a party at the Gate. There were a lot of people there, and they were all drunk. Several strangers were there, too. I sat down and drank a Coke and talked to my friends. Charlie came down and joined our conversation. Out of the clear blue sky, a drunken girl I never saw before started screaming at me and came toward me. She waved her arms and yelled at me and tried to punch me. Charlie got in front of me, grabbed her, took her outside and dragged her to the Gate and threw her out! He yelled for the Gate to be closed and told her she is permanently barred from the Gate! He returned to me and asked if I was OK. I said yes, but I was still in shock. I couldn't believe what happened! I wasn't doing or saying anything wrong. What was her problem? Charlie was angry. He picked up his drink and took a sip. He said "She's always been trouble! She comes here every year and starts a bunch of s---! Sandy didn't do anything! I mean it—C.—is barred!" He looked to Harold and said, "Make sure you tell all the guards and everyone who knows her that she's not allowed in! Never!" He took a deep breath, gently patted my shoulder, and sat down. We all started talking and had a good time. I knew I still loved Charlie. He saved me from that lunatic! He was my hero! What a way to start a new year!

1974

JANUARY 1, 1974   Elvis went to a party last night. Some people followed him.

JANUARY 2, 1974   Woke up to an ice storm! Horrible. This is the worse it has been since 1953. Glad I didn't work. Didn't go to the Gate, either—they called to tell me Elvis was riding his snowmobile up and down the driveway! I missed it!

JANUARY 6, 1974   It was announced that Elvis will do a concert in Memphis for the first time in 13 years, and it's on my birthday! I'm so excited!

JANUARY 7, 1974   65 degrees! What a change in weather!

JANUARY 8, 1974   Elvis' birthday. Thank God, he didn't marry Linda.

JANUARY 12, 1974   Announced Elvis will do a second show in Memphis! I mailed my check. I should get a seat for one of the shows.

JAUARY 13, 1974   Another show was announced! No personal checks are accepted! I bought a money order and mailed it. Pray I'm not too late! The shows are SOLD OUT.

JANUARY 16, 1974   Israel signed a peace treaty.

JANUARY 18, 1974   Bon and I went to Shoneys for dinner. Vernon Presley was there with a young blonde. I don't know who she is.

JANUARY 21, 1974   Mom's birthday. I miss her so much. Our cousin is living with her and Dad until the baby is born.

JANUARY 28, 1974   I have been so sick with a sore throat and depressed. Got Elvis pictures from Aileen in Ireland. One is from Vegas, 1969. The others are from the Hawaiian special right off her TV! They turned out great!! It helped brighten my day. Beautiful!

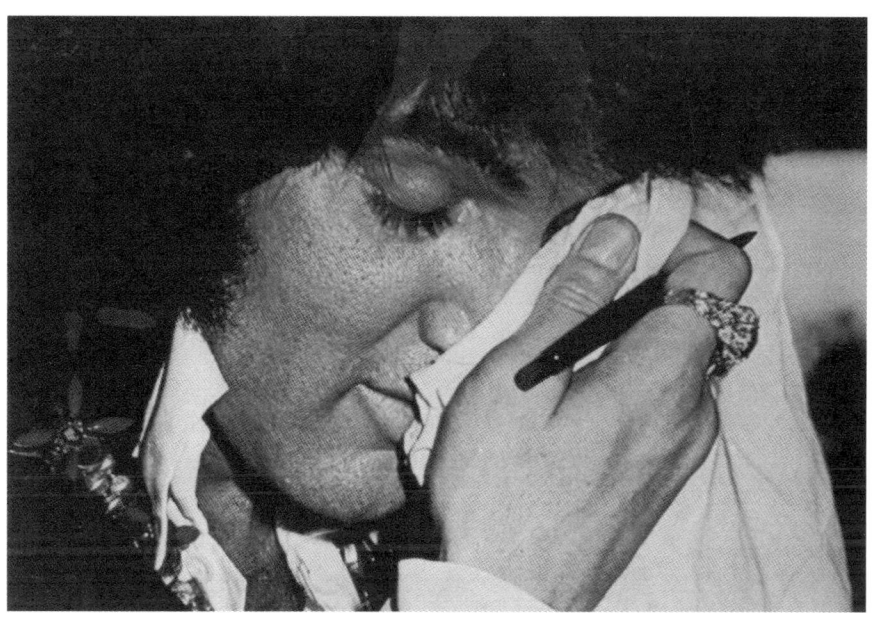

JANUARY 29, 1974   Concert tickets will not be sent out for 3 weeks! Guess they didn't expect so many tickets to sell so fast!

JANUARY 30, 1974   Traded my days off so I can go to KY and visit Mom and Dad.

FEBRUARY 1, 1974   Went to KY. Dad is putting an indoor toilet in for Mammy. She's so old, and it's too dangerous to go to the outhouse! Mom agreed to the name of Kelly Jo for my new sister. She insists it's a boy and he'll be named Jason.

FEBRUARY 4, 1974   Mom and Dad left for Ind. the same time I left for Memphis. I started crying in my car. I know I'll miss them. I wanted to turn around and go with them, but I went home.

FEBRUARY 13, 1974   Got my Elvis concert tickets! They sent me a ticket for both nights! Since my check was from a Memphis bank, it was accepted! They're both on the first floor! Saturday is in the 3rd row! Sunday is a little farther back! I can't believe it! I'll be so close! Elvis hands out scarves and kisses girls that go to the stage. I hope I can get one or both.

FEBRUARY 15, 1974   Called the Gate. Harold said Elvis will be home any day now. Linda has been back a couple days.

FEBRUARY 15, 1974   Got Elvis' "Legendary Album."

FEBRUARY 18, 1974   Linda came down driving Elvis' Stutz. NO ONE drives that car but Elvis!! We were all surprised! Lisa is supposed to have her tonsils removed in a few days.

FEBRUARY 22, 1974   I know security around Graceland is lax, but I would never take advantage. Somehow, a guy walked all the way to the House, knocked on the door and asked if Elvis was home! Of all the nerve! The guards flew up to get the guy and make him leave. I hope Elvis doesn't find out. I don't want the Gate to be barred to all of us fans.

MARCH 3, 1974   I love my job as a long distance operator! Placed a person to person call to Red West! Guy who answered said they already left for the concert. I got the phone numbers to the hotel and the House! My little secret!!

MARCH 10-15, 1973   Vacation in Ind. Good to see my family. Baby Kelly/Jason is not born yet. I have been so depressed for so long. Don't know what's wrong. In a way, I want to stay here, but I'll see Elvis and Charlie tomorrow! We celebrated my birthday.

MARCH 16, 1974   My birthday! Left Chicago in the rain and it was raining in Memphis. Bon picked me up at the airport. I wore my new, floor length, blue dress. Got to the theater in plenty of time. I was escorted to the 3rd row! The only bad thing is I was in the center, so I couldn't get out to the stage for a scarf!

Saw Red and Sonny West, Ricky Stanley, and Lamar is back! Also saw Col. Parker. Linda was there. She wore an ugly outfit made of strings of mink! Awful! Her hair was bleached and she looked prettier than I'd seen her, except that dress!

Charlie came on stage about 8:00. He was tuning his guitar. I went to the stage to see him. It had been raised 6' for security reasons. I couldn't reach the top. I called his name and he moved closer to me. The lights were too bright for him to recognize me. I told him who I was. He smiled and sat down. He was glad I was there. He looked so handsome. It was good to see him smile. We talked for a while. I asked if I could take a picture. He said sure, he stood, held up his guitar, and posed for me. The picture is beautiful! The show was going to start, so he had to leave. I was so excited! I went back to my seat and wondered if I could somehow get to the stage. I wanted a scarf and a kiss from Elvis! An announcement was made on the radio and again before the show started that extra security was hired. NO ONE would be allowed out of his seat or to approach the stage! If he did, security would escort him out!

I waited impatiently for the show to begin. Finally, the lights dimmed and a comedian was introduced. He performed for about 20 minutes. The Sweet Inspirations came out to sing. They are all so very talented. I wonder if they know how lucky they are to work with Elvis. I'm sure they do. Intermission.

The lights dimmed. The audience was silent. The music started. Everyone was quiet. All eyes were on the stage. No introduction was needed! Everyone knew Elvis was coming out! The spotlight shined. The flashbulbs went off. The room was all lit up. There he was! He walked to his mike and grabbed it. He kept looking around. He wore a white jumpsuit decorated with beads and spangles, but no cape. He had gained a little weight, but he still looked good. His hair wasn't as dry as it had been. He seemed so nervous, but he started singing "Teddy Bear."

After a couple songs, he stopped, drank some water, and looked out at the audience. "I see they raised the stage up high. I know they said no one was to come to the stage. But, guess what? You're my fans. You made me what I am. Without you, I'd be driving a truck. If you want to come up, come on up! And security, you'd better not hurt anyone!" The audience roared! It was like a dare! I couldn't believe how many girls ran to the stage. I was frightened! They were even climbing over me! There was no way I would get in that horrible crowd! I sat listening to every song and took pics. I realized I hardly watched Elvis! I was too busy with my camera!

He sang most of the same songs as in 1972 and sang "Steamroller Blues," "Why Me Lord?" and "Help Me." Most of what he did was the same as Chicago—girl calling him and he said he'd be up later. My greatest birthday present ever! I love him and Charlie! The concert lasted over 2 hours. Elvis sang for over an hour. No encore. Again the announcement: "Elvis has left the building."

It took forever to get outside. I finally reached my car. I decided to drive around in case Elvis hadn't left yet. He wasn't there. I sighed and went home with happy thoughts of the show. I'll get my scarf and kiss tomorrow!

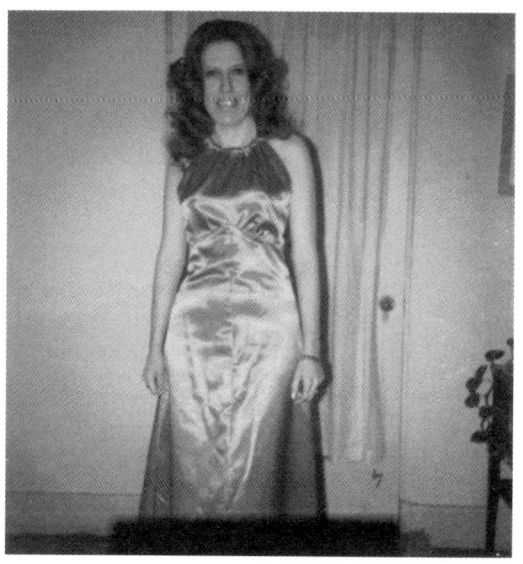

MARCH 17, 1974   My seat was about 10 rows from the stage and on the aisle. I tried to reach the stage, but the crowd was too thick and security wouldn't let me by. I was disappointed and angry—they let all the other girls go by! But, I took pics and tried to tape the show. I couldn't see well enough to operate it, so I didn't get any of the songs.

Linda was there again. I thought the dress last night was horrible—this one was hideous! Black and different colored streamers! Yuck! I thought of asking for a picture and started to approach her. Some others reached her first, and then she started talking to her parents. I decided the heck with it.

Elvis sang the same songs. I enjoyed it more tonight and paid attention. He wore a blue jumpsuit. Blue is his color! He was much more at ease tonight. He thanked all his fans, especially everyone in Memphis for all they had done for him. He sang the same songs, but that was fine with me.

I wish I could witness to him. I went to the Gate. Elvis didn't go home tonight or last night. He stayed at the Rivermont Hotel.

Harold got a golf cart and drove me around the House again. We sat at the pool and Meditation Garden. We had the run of the place! I even used the bathroom there again! Not many people can say that! Elvis is leaving for another tour in a couple days.

MARCH 18, 1974   Elvis did another concert that had been added due to all the tickets sold. I didn't have a ticket, so I couldn't go.

MARCH 19, 1974   Went to the Coleseum after the concert with hopes I would see Elvis leaving the concert. When I arrived, he had just entered the black limo and sat in the back seat. I didn't see him. Liz and I followed his car to the airport. We got to see Elvis board the plane. He stopped, waved, and blew kisses to us before he entered the plane. We watched as he flew off. Wasn't enough time to grab my camera and take pics.

MARCH 21, 1974   Elvis went to Nashville to hide from the crowds. He'll be home tomorrow.

MARCH 22, 1974   Went to the Gate. Harold's truck was repossessed. Elvis bought him a new one! Elvis' car came down the driveway slowly about 12:30. Sonny was driving. Elvis and Linda were in the back seat. Elvis turned around and waved to me. Linda turned and surprisingly, she waved to me, and I waved back. They went to the Memphian. The show was closed.

MARCH 24, 1974   Elvis didn't go anywhere. He has a new guy names Al working for him. Charlie didn't go out, so I haven't talked to him for some time.

MARCH 25, 1974   Got my concert pictures back. They are so small! It looks like I was a mile away from him. Oh, well.

MARCH 26, 1974   I was nominated as a leader of a ladies group at church, but I declined, as I don't feel I can devote enough time for that. Elvis left for Calif. I missed seeing him, as I was waiting at the Memphian.

March 31, 1974   I bought Elvis' new album "Good Times." It's the one he was recording at Stax. Went to the Gate. The Mach IV was in front of the House.

APRIL 1, 1974 Elvis and Linda had a big fight. He left and hasn't been home.

April 4, 1974 Tom went to see Don Henning, an Elvis impersonator. Tom didn't like him. Linda was there. She liked Don and wants Vernon to see him.

APRIL 6, 1974 Called Mom. The baby still isn't born, but has dropped quite a bit. Elvis turned down a $1 million concert in Australia! And an Easter concert was cancelled. Don't know what's happening.

APRIL 7, 1974 Called Harold. Elvis isn't home yet. I know it's terrible, but I wish he'd get rid of Linda. She's so stuck up. I don't know what he sees in her. She's staying at the House.

APRIL 12, 1974 Elvis is home, but he didn't go anywhere. Charlie came down. A girl ran to him and they talked for a minute. He left. Didn't get to talk to him.

APRIL 15, 1974 Bon and I went to look at apartments. near the church. She wants to move, but I don't know if we can afford it. We'd have to buy furniture. She can barely make the rent where we are. We're praying about it. I had my credit checked, and I can buy furniture from the store!

Elvis went out and Linda wasn't with him. Went to the Memphian and Crosstown, but I couldn't find him. Judy brought her baby to the Gate. Charlie stopped his car and held her. He talked baby talk and smiled. I took a picture. Felt strange to see him with a baby. He'd be a good daddy.

APRIL 17, 1974 Bon called about the apartment. If a couple doesn't take it, we'll have it.

APRIL 18, 1974 We got the apartment! I went to the bank to get the money and took the deposit. It's $110.00 a month plus utilities. It has 2 big bedrooms, a bath with a tub and shower, living room, dining area. The kitchen is furnished with a gas stove, dishwasher, fridge, and a garbage disposal. It's fully carpeted. There is a swimming pool, a tennis court, and a laundramat. It's so nice. We will have to cut back on eating out and some other things. But, the Lord wants us here, or we wouldn't have gotten it.

APRIL 22, 1974 Called to get the utilities and phone set up for the new place. My furniture will be delivered in a few days. Packed. Excited!

Went to the Gate. Elvis sneaked out the back way, but we spotted his car. Pat, Shirley, and I got in my car and followed him. We knew he was heading to the Memphian, so I passed him and decided to beat him there. He passed me and I couldn't catch up. When we reached the building, he jumped out of his car and ran inside before we could even get out of my car. We didn't get any pictures. We were mad! We decided to wait for him to come out. We discussed what we would say to him. We wanted to write a note to give him telling him we were hurt that he ran in. We were the only ones there! Why did he run?

About 15 minutes later, I glanced up and saw the side door to the theater open. Elvis and a group of guys ran out and were running toward us. I jumped out of my car and said, "It's Elvis! He's coming!" I turned my head to look at the girls. I yelled, "Hurry! Elvis is coming!" I turned my head and said, "Elvis is HERE!" He stopped just a few feet in front of me. Some of the guys were with him. Some were looking at the Mach IV. He kept looking around for something or someone. I was shocked! I didn't know what to say. Should I ask what was wrong? Should I ask what they were looking for? I was nervous. The only thing I could say was: "Elvis, may I have a picture with you? Please?" He kept looking around. "Not now, Hon. Later."

The guys had been running around the theater. They joined Elvis and said they didn't find anyone. Elvis said something about the car to the guys, but I couldn't understand what he said. I knew it was about the car, so I said, "Elvis, we would NEVER do anything to hurt you or your car." He continued looking around. "I know, Honey. It was someone else and we're trying to find them." We were asked if we had seen anyone around the car. We told them the truth: NO! Red West told us someone called the theater to warn Elvis that hippies were messing with his car. We told Elvis we hadn't seen anyone else, and it wasn't us. He said, "OK. If you see anyone, let us know." We promised we would. Elvis turned around and went back into the building.

Red questioned us. He never said it, but I sensed he was insinuating we were the ones who called. I kept telling him it wasn't us! Elvis was so nice to me, but Red was being snotty. Finally, one of the guys came from the front of the theater with two girls-- C and J. (C was the one who had tried to beat me up at the Gate!) "I found them hiding in the phone booth on the corner!" C pointed at us and said, "They were messing with Elvis' car! We called to warn Elvis!" Pat, Shirley, and I denied it! Red shook his head and started yelling at C and J. He was really mad. He said, "C, you were told to stay away from Elvis! Why are you here?"

C and J were scared. They knew they were caught. They confessed. "We only wanted to talk to Elvis." They assumed he'd exit from the front door and were waiting for him. They were surprised when he came over to us!

Red told C and J to leave, and not to come back. He told them to never pull a trick like that again. If they did, they would be put in jail. The only reason why the cops weren't called was cuz no damage had been done to the car!

We watched C and J run to their car. The motor started, tires squealed, and the car sped by. Red said, "That's them. They're gone." He looked at me. I thought he'd apologize, but he didn't. "Let us know if they come back." We said we would. He and the guy went back into the theater. The door closed.

We waited a while and decided to go back to the Gate. We talked about all that happened. They couldn't believe I actually spoke to Elvis and that he spoke to me! They wished they had said something, but they were too scared to say anything except we didn't do anything! Shirley wanted to know why Elvis referred to me as Honey. He never called her Honey. She was upset cuz they were neighbors and she had known Elvis for many years. I told her I didn't think he knew my name. (But, Charlie knew my name without being introduced to me. Maybe Elvis had heard it and didn't remember? I hoped). Afterward, I realized that every time he talked to me, he always called me Honey. I felt honored. The man I love calls me Honey! Elvis wore blue slacks, a black shirt, and a blue scarf around his neck. Since he had been running, his hair was down on his face. His eyes were puffy and he looked tired. But, he was still beautiful and so nice to me. I was happy, even though I didn't get a picture!

APRIL 24, 1974   Elvis mood has sure changed. He sneaks out the back way and avoids the fans. Shirley and I met with Charlie to see what the problem is. We told him that if Elvis doesn't want us around, we won't bother him anymore. Charlie said that's not true. Elvis is under a lot of emotional problems. He told us the shows were all closed to fans for security reasons-- Elvis is getting a lot of death threats and they don't want to take a chance. We talked for over an hour.

APRIL 27, 1974   David Stanley got married. Elvis attended;

he was gone before I got to the Gate. Pat and I went to the Memphian, but Elvis didn't show. Learned later some people followed him to a racquetball club. He posed for pictures. I was too tired, so I went home. I was hurt that no one called to tell me where he was or I would have gone. Learned there were a lot of personality conflicts at the Gate. I may not go there again.

APRIL 29, 1974   Two girls from KY asked me to take them to the Memphian to see Elvis. They had never seen him, so I said OK. We waited for over 2 hours before the cars drove up. We went to them. Elvis was wearing an orange jumpsuit. He and the guys walked to the theater. Joe Espisito stood in front of Elvis to block him. "No pictures! Get back!" We all did. Elvis said, "I just finished playing ball and I'm a mess. Please, don't take any pictures." One of the girls asked if we could have autographs. Joe said, "No!" Elvis sounded disgusted and said. "All right." The girls found paper and a pen and handed them to Elvis. Joe was mad! I was mad with Elvis' attitude! He had posed for pictures the past 3 nights. There were only 3 of us girls! I just stood there and watched. Elvis kept looking up at me. I said, "I have one already. I don't want to bother you." Elvis stared at me as he went down the stairs to the theater. He entered the door, stopped, turned around and looked at me strangely—like he didn't believe what I said and acted the way I did. He entered, and the door closed.

MAY 1, 1974   The phone rang at 9:00 AM. It was Mom. I have a baby brother named Jason! He was born at 5:24, weighs 7 lbs 6 oz 20" long and has blonde hair. I'm so excited! I did want a sister, but I know I'll love Jason even more! Got everything moved into the new apartment. Got to sleep in my new bed! So good to be in a place with no mice, a new brother, new furniture! I'm so happy!

MAY 2, 1974   Alan from the Gate has been teasing me and trying to get me to go to bed with him. Harold said Alan told him I've been chasing and begging him to go to bed. I hope these rumors stop! Mom called. She got to take Jason home from the hospital. I can't wait to see him. She says he's the prettiest baby she ever saw—except for me.

MAY 3, 1974   Several of Elvis' guys have been stopping at the Gate and taking girls up to the House. I admit I'm jealous. But, the girls all confessed that they slept with the guy who took them up. Some of them saw Elvis, but most didn't. The guys start the visit by asking the girls to remove their shoes (Elvis has a foot fetish and I guess the guys act like they do, too) so they can rub the girl's feet. One thing leads to another, then another. That's not for me. I would love to be in the House and talk to Elvis and the others about religion. No sex for me until I marry!

MAY 4, 1974   I wore my hot pants suit to the Gate. Elvis returned home at 4:00 AM. Elvis' stepbrother, Billy, kept going in and out of the Gate. He stopped on his way in, stared at me, threw a cigarette toward me, and went up to the House. I was tired and decided to go home. As I walked toward my car, the House phone rang. I gave my usual joking response: "Tell him I'll be right up!" I was referring to Elvis calling down for me. Harold and everyone there yelled for me to come back—Billy was on the phone and wanted to talk to me. I said, "Yeah, right!" I continued to my car. Pat and Liz came and got me. They literally drug me to the shack. I figured: OK. I'll go along with the joke. I picked up the phone and a voice said, "Hi, Sandy. It's Billy. Would you like to come up and talk for a while?" I was so surprised! I thought about what the girls had said the past couple weeks. I took a deep breath, tried to remain calm. "OK. But just to talk." He agreed.

I was leery about going up, but Pat and Liz said I should go up just to see the House. Besides, Elvis might show up and I'd miss him. A few minutes later, Billy came down on a golf cart. He drove me to the House. We entered through the back entrance. It was like a dream. We went through the lounge and he took me down some stairs to the basement. The stairs and walls were covered with red, velvet carpeting. Somewhere along the way we passed the laundry room. We went through a room with a piano and a pool table. The room wasn't as big as I had imagined. We passed a room that had different statues, etc. I saw the long couch Harold had told me about. It is so big it wouldn't fit in any of the doors. The deliverers had to remove the picture window, bring in the couch, and return the window to its place.

We went to the den. It was beautiful! All the lights were turned off, except for some long lights across the back wall. We continued walking. There was a bar with lots of glasses hanging from the ceiling. It was all black leather. Mirrors covered the three corner walls. There was a wall that slightly separated the bar from the rest of the room. A large, thick, red shag rug covered nearly the whole floor. On the back wall there was a stereo, built in juke box, record player, radio, and 3 built in TV sets all in a row. Billy said Elvis watches all 3 sets at the same time during football season to see all the games at once.

On the left side of the room was a huge gas fire place with limestone on the back wall. Billy turned it on. It was beautiful. I told him I love fire places. I saw white, modern art sculpture of a man and a woman. Next to it were 2 chairs. A telephone and stand were beside them. Records were on the floor next to the fireplace. Two chairs sat on the opposite side of the room. They were white with a green flower decoration and sat along the wall. Pictures of a lake hung on the wall opposite the chairs. There was a sculpture of a peacock, 2 huge white chairs with green flowers. A little end table was next to the chairs, a matching coffee table was in the center of the room. Artificial flowers were throughout the whole room. There was a small bathroom on the left.

We sat down on the floor across from each other. He removed his shoes and asked me to remove mine. I explained that the boots were too hard for me to put back on. I thought, "Oh, boy! Here we go!" I put my guard up. Billy began talking about all the things we could do in the future—swim in the pool, play football, attend the movies, etc., if we went to bed together. I politely explained that I am a Christian and believe sex is for a man and his wife only. We talked a little about Elvis and I brought up religion. He listened. He didn't get fresh and was nice enough.

I kept looking around to see if Elvis was coming, but he didn't. Billy said he had gone to bed. We talked a little more, and I said I was tired and needed to go home. First, I had to use the restroom. I was so thrilled to be in the House again! This time in the rooms—not just the area where Elvis got his hair cut and where people changed clothes to swim.

I heard Billy talking to someone, but I didn't know whom. I finished, washed and dried my hands, and rejoined Billy. We went back upstairs and outside to the golf cart. He drove me down to the Gate zig-zagging through the trees—lights turned off.

Harold stood outside the shack grinning ear to ear, his arms crossed in front. "I told you, Billy," Harold said. Billy didn't say anything to him. Billy and I said goodnight. I thanked him for taking me to the House. He nodded and left.

Harold told me Billy called him while I was in the bathroom. He asked Harold what the hell was going on. Harold told him "I told you she's not like the others." Harold looked at me and laughed. "You are the only girl I know who went to the House and didn't sleep with anyone! I can't believe it!"

Harold, Pat and Liz were the only ones there. I excitedly described the House and told them what happened. Pat and Liz were as excited as I! I had been awake for over 24 hours and decided I'd better go home.

I was so tired and excited. I prayed I wouldn't fall asleep while driving home. I was glad we now lived a mile or so away and not on the other side of town. Bon was asleep. I didn't wake her. I'd tell her later. I went to bed at 8:00 AM. I thanked God for allowing me entrance to the House and for keeping me safe. I had witnessed to Billy. I'll probably never know whether he listened or not. I had done what God wanted me to do. Well, Billy and I can still be friends.

MAY 4, 1974   Bon came crying to me at 10 AM. Her dad was in the hospital emergency room in Indiana. A main artery in his stomach burst and he was losing blood. They were waiting for the doctors to come to perform surgery. They didn't take him to surgery until 4PM. At 8 PM, the family called Bon and asked her to come home. They didn't expect her dad to live through the night.

I had money to give her for a plane ticket. Thank God the airport was only a few minutes away. We made good time. I searched for a parking place at the airport. As I started to pull in, a woman ran a yield sign and hit my car! The impact was so great that Bon was thrown forward. Her head hit and broke the front windshield! (I told her before we left to put on the seat belt, but she didn't.) She was bleeding.

Airport security was notified somehow. It seemed like forever before they arrived. They checked to be sure we were all OK. When they saw Bon, they wanted to call an ambulance. She was crying so hard she couldn't talk. I explained the situation to them. They called the cops. I kept telling them Bon HAD to catch a flight! After the cops investigated and got all the insurance information, they drove Bon up to the airport and stayed with her until she caught a plane. Security stayed with me until I finally calmed down some.

My car was drivable, so I went home. The phone was ringing as I entered the apt. It was Midge, the preacher's wife. Bon had called and told her what had happened. She asked Midge to check on me and take me to their home for the night. Bless her heart. She was worried about me. And, I was worrying about HER! Later, Bon called. She was able to see her dad before he passed away. I'm grateful she made the trip on time and safely, but so sad about her dad.

I slept in one of the kid's bunk beds. I couldn't believe how I could be so excited the night before and so sad now. I cried myself to sleep.

MAY 5, 1974   I attended church, but I asked one of the girls to teach Sunday school for me. I convinced Midge and J D that I was OK and went home. I was glad I did! The fridge broke down. Water from the freezer was on the floor! All the food in the freezer was ruined. Thank God, we didn't have too much in it.

MAY 6, 1974   The police report hasn't been submitted to my insurance company yet. I have to wait for them to receive it before I can file a claim. Mom was notified by Bon's family of what happened. She called to check on me. She wants me to move to Ind. NOW! I told her I can't. I have to take care of business here first.

MAY 12, 1974   Bon came back. She's doing OK. She does NOT want to move back to Ind.! I was afraid she would. She gave me a picture of Jason. He's a beautiful baby. I can't wait to see him.

MAY 17, 1974   I started crocheting a blanket for Jason. Hope to get it done before I see him. It's variable blue. I love the color.

MAY 20, 1974 $800.00 damage on my car. They'll work on it next week.

MAY 27, 1974   Mom and Dad called. I traded days off and will fly to Ind. this weekend. My car is fixed. Can't wait to see Jason!

MAY 31, 1974   I fell in love with Jason the moment I saw him! He is so beautiful and sweet! Hazel will finish the blanket for me. Danny is back in Indiana and wants to see me. I told Hazel again there's no way!

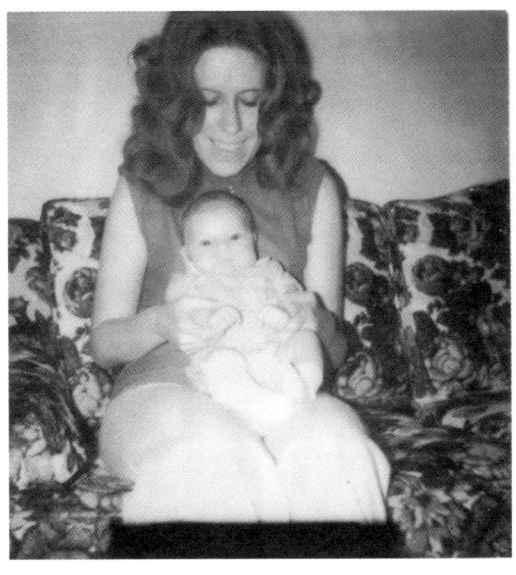

JUNE 1, 1974	Got to see all my family. Went to church and saw all my old friends. Jason has a club foot and may have to have surgery to correct it. I wish Mom and Dad would move to Memphis. I miss them so much. And now we have Jason to look after.

JUNE 5, 1974	I placed a long distance personal call to singer Tony Joe White at work. (He sang the hit song "Polk Salad Annie") I got to hear his voice as he said hello. I love being an operator! Get all kinds of calls! Elvis isn't home yet.

JUNE 6, 1974	Talked to Vester. He said Elvis is trying to get rid of Linda, but she won't leave. Elvis is not home, but Linda is here.

JUNE 10, 1974	Bon got her furniture. The place is all furnished now!

JUNE 20, 1974	Elvis is still not home. President Nixon returned from the Mideast. So many people want him impeached because of Watergate.

JUNE 21, 1974	Linda was moved OUT of the House! Vester said it took 3 car loads to get all her stuff out! Her parents helped her move. Even her dog is gone.

JUNE 26, 1974	President Nixon is going to Moscow. I've been tanning by the pool, but it's starting to fade cuz it has rained the past couple days.

JUNE 29, 1974	Met Mom and Dad in KY. Jason sure has grown! He's so sweet.

JUNE 30, 1974	Dad changed my oil and one of my tires before I left for Memphis. I'll miss them. The mother of Dr. Martin Luther King, Jr. was killed as she worshipped in church. Hope there won't be any rioting.

JULY 2, 1974	Linda is back. Don't know what happened.

JULY 4, 1974   Elvis is back. He went to the show and posed for pictures. I missed it.

JULY 5, 1974   Elvis came down on the golf cart. He was racing with some of the guys and actor Chuck Norris! Got a lot of pictures of him. Thought he was going to hit someone! Later, I followed him to the show in Whitehaven. Saw him when he went in and out. Linda wore a long, white dress and wrap around shoes. They didn't stay long. Learned later a guy was found sitting in the living room of the House on the couch waiting for Elvis! He was arrested. I don't know how these people sneak in. The guards didn't know, either. I'm afraid they might lose their jobs.

JULY 6, 1974   Elvis and Linda rode golf carts. He didn't drive so fast this time. I had my camera up. He smiled at me and I took a picture. He went up to the House and sneaked out in his new jeep and went to the Memphian.

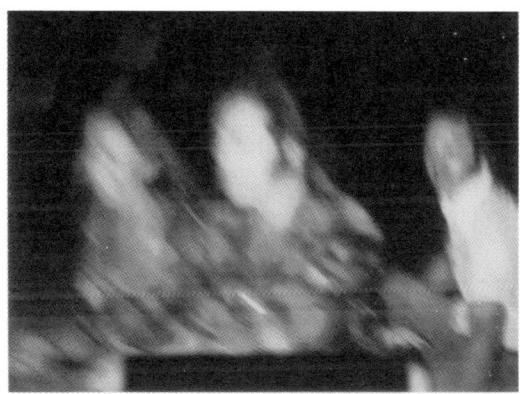

JULY 7, 1974   Tony's birthday. Elvis didn't go out. He has been staying in his bedroom. I hope he's not sick again. Harold let us go up to the House and walk around again. Heard a woman's voice screaming: "Help! Help!" I looked at Harold stunned that he didn't go see what was happening. He laughed and told me it was Elvis' pet peacock!

JULY 8, 1974   A girl from England had been in Memphis several days and never got to see Elvis. She's going home tomorrow. I took her to the Memphian. Elvis was in a bad mood. He rushed into the theater, so we only got a glimpse of him. The girl was glad to see him but disappointed it was so fast. The Gate has been closed for about a week to everyone—even the regulars—since the guy sneaked in the House. Elvis' stepbrother, Ricky, destroyed a political sign and had been arrested. Elvis paid the bail. That's probably why he was so mad.

JULY 9, 1974   The Gate is closed. Only 5 people are allowed in at a time. The ones there now had been there all day. They refused to leave and let someone else in. I was mad!

JULY 10, 1974   The telephone company is talking about going on strike. Both sides are still talking. I pray we won't. Not sure how long it would last. Ricky was arrested for the sign damage again. Elvis is furious. He didn't go out.

JULY 12, 1974   Went to the Gate. Someone stole gas from Elvis' white Caddy. They don't know who or where, but David thinks it's funny.

JULY 13, 1974   Followed Elvis to the Memphian. His car was there, but he didn't get out. We ran to the front to wait for him. Someone spotted him on the other side of the building. As we headed that way, Elvis was running the opposite direction and nearly ran into me! He ran to the front door and tried to open it, but it was locked. There were about 10 of us fans there, none of his guys. He turned his back to us, placed both hands on the building and hid his face. He was only 3 feet away from me. I wanted to get a picture, but I knew he didn't want that. I sensed he was scared. The door finally opened and he went in. He was dressed completely in white and was barefoot! Learned later that all the doors were locked and he couldn't get in! Glad no one tried to hurt him.

JULY 15, 1974   Linda drove the car out. Elvis was in the passenger side. He had bandages on his hands. Don't know what happened.

JULY 17, 1974   Followed Elvis to the Memphian and waited for him to come out. April was gonna ask for a pic, but she chickened out. When he came out, he looked weird. He kept staring at us like we were crazy. No one said a word to him. He got in the car and left. Someone in the group said Elvis was drunk. He didn't seem to be to me, but he did look strange.

JULY 18, 1974   As we followed Elvis to the Memphian in my car, we (Pauline, April, and I) were right behind Elvis' car all the way across town. A traffic light turned red. Charlie's car was in front. Elvis was behind him, then me. Both cars stopped. I was in a goofy mood and said, "Let's ignore Elvis and pretend we don't know who he is." I drove my car to the side of Charlie, beeped, and we all waved to him. He was surprised and happy to see us. He beeped and waved back. Elvis flashed his headlights, beeped, smiled and waved to us. We waved back. When the light changed, Charlie took off. I was still waiting. Elvis drove by me, beeped and waved. All the rest of the way, he and I took turns slowing down, speeding up, and passing and waving. It was so funny! I was glad Elvis was in a good mood.

Elvis was in the theater before we got out of my car. We waited for him to come out. April asked Elvis if we could take pictures. He said, "Well. Allright." April ran to him and I readied my camera. "Should I take you or Elvis?" I joked. Elvis snickered. "Both of us," he said. I snapped it, pulled the Polaroid film out and waited for April to come take mine next. I handed the photo and the camera to her and started toward Elvis. Out of nowhere, a group of girls came running toward Elvis. "I have to go," Elvis said. "Later, Honey." He ran and got in his car and drove off. I sighed and figured I'd try again tomorrow.

On the way back to the Gate, we asked to see the picture. April, who is ditzy, said, "Oh, no!" I thought she lost it! "It's stuck to my drivers' license!" My heart stopped. She slowly separated it. I pulled the car over and we waited. Thank God, the only thing destroyed was the lower left side and only a small portion! Elvis was in perfect condition! He wore black pants, a white shirt, and blue vest. Pauline and I were so angry that those girls popped up so fast. Wish they hadn't been there!

JULY 19, 1974   April called. She left her purse in my car. I took the picture to the drugstore to get prints made. April was angry! She didn't want anyone to have a copy! She kept saying it was HER picture! I told her I took it with my camera and I wanted a copy at least for me! I hope it turns out good. Mom called. Jason had surgery on his clubbed foot. All went well. He will wear a cast for a while. Mom and Dad will go to court Wednesday to get legal custody of Jason.

JULY 20, 1974   We vote next week at work on whether or not to strike. I hope not. I can't afford it. Don't know how long it would last.

JULY 21, 1974   Leta wants to start a fan club for Charlie. Charlie took her to the House. She said Elvis came down and talked to them for 3 hrs!

JULY 22, 1974   Elvis pulled out of the Gate and turned right on the hwy. We were behind him and he suddenly made an illegal U turn. As he passed my car, he stared at me—I could see he was embarrassed. He headed toward the Crosstown Theater. He stopped at a green light and we stopped behind him. When the light turned red, he took off! I was so tired. I just gave upand went home.

JULY 23, 1974   Harold told us Elvis posed for pictures again last night! Pauline and I are so mad. It seems it's always when I'm not there. I'll wait and see what happens tomorrow.

Harold sneaked Pauline and me up to the House. We peeked in the windows at Elvis new furniture—all African style. UGLY!! Harold took us around and got us some of the old and new carpet that was just laid. Both are red. We vote next Fri. on whether or not to strike.

JULY 24, 1974   Mom called—Jason is legally ours! I thank God for that!

April, Pauline, Pat and I went to a Waylon Jennings concert. We saw a group of guys walk behind the stage. We wanted to meet Waylon, so we followed them. The door was open to a room where the guys were standing. It was Waylon's dressing room. They were joking and having drinks. April asked which one was Waylon. I didn't know—they all had beards and I never saw him with one. So, April, in her pushy style and loud voice, screamed, "Waylon!" I was embarrassed. He turned around and faced us. "Yes?" he said. "That's him." April said and began walking toward him. She asked if we could have pictures and autographs. He said yes and invited us in. We were offered drinks and snacks and sat down. The guys were discussing the show and tuning their instruments. We sat quietly in a corner. Waylon said, "Look at those pretty girls! I think they're scared of us!" I finally got enough nerve to speak. I explained that we are Elvis fans and when we are around him we are warned to be quiet and not disturb anyone. They laughed.

Waylon grabbed his guitar, sat down on a couch, and invited us to sit with him. He and the guys started jamming—it was so cool! He posed for pictures, signed autographs, and kissed us all on the cheek. We were there for about ½ hr. He stood and asked if we were staying for the show. We nodded. He told us to sit up front so he could sing to us. He nicely explained they had to get dressed for the show and asked us to step out. He walked us to the door and said, "I'm sorry. I hope y'all understand. But, you are more than welcome to come back after the show. In fact, I hope you do. We can jam some more and have a good time." We thanked him and went to the auditorium. We couldn't believe how nice he was! We all even commented on how we wish Elvis was more like that to us. Elvis had seen us hundreds of times—Waylon hadn't!

We got seats, ordered Cokes, and waited for the show to start. It was fabulous! So many good country songs! Such a talent! It was over too soon. We went backstage later to thank him and tell him how great he was. Not sure how long we chatted, listened to him sing and play. But, we were very impressed. One of us checked the time and decided we should head for the Gate. We explained to Waylon that we didn't want to miss seeing

Elvis. We even invited him to come along! But, he had another show to do. He hugged and kissed us goodbye and we were off.

We talked about it all the way to the Gate. The Gates were closed cuz of the large crowds. Only the regulars were allowed inside. We yelled for Harold to open the Gate. He did, and we entered. So many sighs and "Who are they?" It was embarrassing but I felt important to be allowed entrance. Went inside the shack and showed the pictures, and shared all we had done with Waylon. Everyone was shocked. It was such a good feeling!

After a while, I heard tires squealing and a VERY loud thud! People were screaming and the crowd went to a place in the center of the highway. All traffic stopped. I heard people screaming: "Someone call for an ambulance! Quick!" Harold yelled in to me that a woman had been hit by a car! I was by the phone, so I immediately picked it up and dialed "0" for operator. I was trembling. When the operator answered, I told her who I was, my operator number and asked her to connect me to an ambulance. I knew her and told her what had happened. When the fire dept. answered, I repeated the information. The voice wanted the address I said, "3764 Hwy 51 in Whitehaven. Elvis Presley Boulevard. Right in front of Graceland. Please send an ambulance right away!" I was finally told one was on the way. I hung up and went outside.

A woman was crossing the hwy to come to the Gate. She was carrying her 2 year old son. A speeding car hit her and sent them flying 30-40 feet in the air! She landed on her head! She was unconscious but still alive. The baby died instantly. I opened the Gate. Harold, Pat, Pauline, and I went out (April left for her trailer and didn't stay with us). Two little boys were standing around the crowd and crying. The woman was their mother! I went to them and began talking softly, asking names and so forth. They were on their way home from vacation and their last name was Robinson. Mr. Robinson was at home waiting for them. Their mom wanted to stop to see Elvis. The boys ran safely across the hwy. A car came barreling down the road and hit their mom. They were crying so hard. I took them into the shack and asked for someone to get water to drink. They knew their address and phone number.

When the police and ambulance arrived, I stayed with the boys while Pauline went to the officers. The boys were checked for injuries and then the cops began questioning them. I prayed so hard for them. They were terrified. The ambulance drove away. The person who hit Mrs. Robinson was arrested for drunk driving.

The phone rang from the House. Harold answered it and explained what happened. Shortly after, several of Elvis' guys came down from the House.

Elvis was talking to one of them. He was driving home when he saw the lights and the stopped traffic. He went to the Holiday Inn and checked in for the night. There was no way he could get past that big crowd. Elvis' orders were for the Robinson boys to be taken to the House for the night and until Mr. Robinson arrived. The police politely refused. The kids would be in their custody.

Elvis had one of the Memphis Mafia call the hospital and Dr. Nick to have everything set up for Elvis to pay for all the medical bills. Mrs. Robinson was to receive the very best of care—no matter what the cost. Mr. Robinson was to be contacted as well. He and the boys would be welcome to stay at Graceland for however long it took for Mrs. Robinson to recover. The police agreed to notify the boys' father. I stayed with the boys until Child Services came. They took the boys and gently explained they would be well cared for. Cars were going down the driveway. They were taking clothes and meds to Elvis. He was so upset he needed tranquilizers. I felt so sorry for him. He felt responsible. I realized there was nothing else I could do, so I went home. I prayed all the way.

JULY 25, 1974 I woke early and called the hospital. Mrs. Robinson passed away while in surgery. I cried. I could still see the boys' faces. Elvis is staying at the hotel. He's on tranquilizers still. I was too upset to go to the Gate.

JULY 26, 1974 I am still depressed about the accident. Elvis is at the hotel and sedated. I did not go to the Gate.

JULY 28, 1974 Elvis is home but still upset. He didn't go out. The guys told us that, in addition to all the medical expenses for Mrs. Robinson, he was paying for all the funeral expenses and everything else the family needed.

The company is trying to keep us from striking. I pray we don't. The House Judiciary voted to have President Nixon impeached.

AUGUST 2, 1974 Jason's cast is off. He will need to wear corrective shoes. Tony is going to Iowa to go to school. Elvis sneaked out the back way. Didn't see him until he left the Memphian. I headed for the Gate. Elvis came up behind me and turned on his bright lights. I was in the right lane, so he could have passed me. I slowed down and so did he. He stayed behind me all the way to the Gate, blinked his lights, beeped, and turned in. Don't know what that was all about.

AUGUST 3, 1974   If the company and Union don't settle, we'll go on strike tomorrow night at 11:00. I pray we don't. Carol, Pauline, and I went to THE PLACE. We danced, met several guys. It was nice, but a bar is NOT the right spot to meet a guy to marry!

AUGUST 4, 1974   It was announced at 11:59 PM at work that the strike had been called off! We waited for a while to be sure. It was true! I'm so happy! Went to the Memphian. I waited until 5:00 for Elvis to come out. I asked him for a picture. He said, "No, thanks." I was furious! I had been through a rough time at work. I couldn't sleep worrying about the strike. I waited nearly 5 hours for Elvis to come out. There were only 3 of us there! This was a slap in the face to me! I thought something I NEVER thought I would: "You can go straight to hell!" I did not say it aloud. I did say angrily, "OK. Don't worry. I won't bother you again." I threw all my stuff into my car, got in, slammed the door, and drove off. I was tired, angry and so hurt! I don't understand why I can't ever get my picture with him!

AUGUST 5, 1974   Pauline called to tell me Elvis watched me in shock as I drove off last night. I'm glad he did! I hate him! I've loved him all these years, and now I hate him! I prayed to God to take my life. I don't want to live! If God doesn't take my life, I'll move back to Indiana

August 8, 1974   Mom called. She and Dad are planning to move to Memphis! They're coming to look for a house and a job for Dad! God answered my prayers! He wants me to stay in Memphis for a reason. Went to the Gate to see Pauline and Pat. They don't understand why I feel this way about Elvis. "There's a very fine line between love and hate," Pauline told me. I don't understand all these emotions inside me. How can I hate the man I've loved all these years? I'm so angry and deeply hurt! I keep praying. President Nixon resigned today! He's the first to ever do that!

AUGUST 9, 1974   Went to get Pauline. She needs a place to stay for a couple weeks til she goes to Vegas for Elvis' shows.

AUGUST 12, 1974   Pauline said Elvis looks awful—he's so bloated and tired.

AUGUST 15, 1974   Mom and Jason are flying down tomorrow. Dad couldn't get off work—he has to finish a job.

AUGUST 16, 1974   Stormed all day and night. Mom's plane couldn't land. They kept circling Memphis for 4 hours. Jason was as white as a sheet when I took him from Mom. He was sick and terrified. Glad they made it safely.

AUGUST 17, 1974   A guy named David that I met last week has called a few times when I wasn't home. He wants to go out. I stubbed my toe on a suitcase. My foot and leg are swollen. Went to the doctor; 2 toes are broken. Had to buy a large shoe to wear and have to keep my leg elevated.

AUGUST 19, 1974   Pauline left for Vegas. She'll stay all month. She worked and saved her money to come here to go to Vegas. I can't afford it. Hope she has a good time.

August 21, 1974   Drove Mom and Jason to KY. Dad will take them home tonight.

AUGUST 27, 1974   Card from Pauline saying how great Elvis is and looks. She's having a great time. She said Elvis is talking more than singing. Talking about the "funky angels" on the ceiling. Joking around with the band and backup singers. Reading the words to the songs. I don't understand it. Hope he's OK.

SEPTEMBER 1, 1974   I'm getting a raise at work! I've been working on my book "Superstar." Hope to get it done, but I'm not good at typing and make a lot of mistakes. Elvis introduced Pris and Lisa and 3 girls at the concert. Linda was not there. Don't know what happened.

SEPTEMBER 8, 1974   Evel Knevel jumped the Grand Canyon on his motorcycle. He didn't make it, but he's OK. Rumors are that Elvis was there to watch. Pauline is back in Memphis. News reports say Elvis is hospitalized with double pneumonia.

SEPTEMBER 10, 1974   A new contract was ratified with the company and Union.

SEPTEMBER 11, 1974   George Klein says Elvis is NOT in the hospital or sick and that he did not go to see Evel. Don't know how the rumors get started.

SEPTEMBER 13, 1974   Shirley called and wanted to see Pauline and me. Went to the Gate. Harold took them up to the House to see the new drapes and remodeling. I stayed at the Gate. I didn't care. Elvis came home home unexpectantly about 5:00 AM. I didn't even look at him. I miss my family.

SEPTEMBER 15, 1974   Elvis came down and flew out of the Gate. He looks awful and is in a bad mood.

September 16, 1974   I took Pauline, Shirley, and her mom to the Memphian. They went to Elvis and started talking to him. I stayed in my car. He was drunk and his voice was slurred. He got in his car and and started driving. He was swerving and couldn't stay on the road. I finally passed him. He turned on his red light and flashed it. Don't know what that was all about.

SEPTEMBER 18, 1974   Pauline called. Elvis went to the Gate and signed autographs. He picked up a girl and took her to the House. She stayed all night. Linda is out of town.

SEPTEMBER 20, 1974   Elvis came down in a new car a couple times. He covered his face with his hand.

SEPTEMBER 22, 1974   Elvis is doing a documentary movie on karate.

SEPTEMBER 30, 1974   Elvis left town. At work I placed a long distance call to Joey Heatherton, an actress.

OCTOBER 4, 1974   Harold called to give me the new telephone number at the Gate. Too many people had gotten it and the line was busy all the time. Only the Regulars were given the new number.

OCTOBER 11, 1974   Talked to Harold. He's writing a book about him and Elvis. Vernon told him not to. We'll see. A jury is being selected for Watergate. President Nixon is ill and can't attend.

OCTOBER 13, 1974   Jason got his first tooth! Bon brought me an article about Elvis. He is being sued for millions of dollars by a guy who claims Elvis beat him up last May.

OCTOBER 18, 1974   I am getting lots of pics of Elvis from all my friends. Harold is trying to find a publisher for his book.

OCTOBER 29, 1974   Letter from Pauline in England. She and her mom had an argument and she moved out. She's staying with 3 girls. President Nixon had surgery.

OCTOBER 20, 1974   Talked to Fred. He's OK. Everything is quiet with Elvis being gone. Jason started crawling and he's talking!

OCTOBER 29, 1974   I have been so depressed this past month. I've been praying that God will show me what to do. Since I'm not interested in seeing Elvis again, I guess I won't be witnessing to him. Mom keeps telling me to move back with them. I asked God to send a man to me who looks like Elvis that I can marry and stay in Memphis, if it's His will.

NOVEMBER 1, 1974   A guy named Lou was leaving an apartment downstairs from me. I had met him and his wife at the Gate. He looks so much like Elvis. He's divorced now and wants to date me. I invited him up for some pop to drink. Bon was mad when she came home. She said we agreed we wouldn't have men in the place alone. I don't remember it. Anyway, Lou and I will get together. He was visiting a friend downstairs when I spotted him. This may be the answer to my prayers!

NOVEMBER 7, 1974   Lou and I have been seeing each other. He asked me to marry him and I said yes! This is the answer from God! He wants me to stay here and be with Lou. Lou was sad that I'll be gone a few days on vacation. He's so tall and handsome! I can't believe he's mine! When he kisses me, my toes curl. I really am in love! I can't wait to tell Mom and Dad!

NOVEMBER 8, 1974   Flew to Ind. for my vacation. Dad picked me up at the airport. Jason sure has grown.

November 20, 1974   Back home. Went to see the person from downstairs who knows Lou. Her name is Margie and she's divorced with 3 small kids. Lou is a wrestler and he's in St. Louis for a wrestling match.

NOVEMBER 28, 1974   Thanksgiving Day. Spent it with Susan's family in Miss. We drove to Ala. Just to say we had been there. Had a good time.

NOVEMBER 29, 1974   Talked to Harold. Elvis did not come home for Thanksgiving—the first time in 20 yrs! He's in Calif. Linda is in Fla. I guess they broke up. No one knows for sure.

DECEMBER 6, 1974   Haven't heard from Lou. Margie isn't home to find out what's going on. I'm confused. Met a guy at the Gate named Buddy. He asked me to see a movie. We'll go this weekend.

DECEMBER 7, 1974   I took some cookies to Margie and her kids. I have a bunch of clothes I was going to give to church. But since Margie is my size, I'll give them to her. She told me Lou is still married! Don't know what to do now!

DECEMBER 9, 1974   Went to the movies with Buddy. He is possessive! I won't go with him again.

DECEMBER 24, 1974   Flew to Ind. for Christmas. Enjoyed being with the family again.

DECEMBER 29, 1974   Flew back to Memphis. Went to the Gate. Elvis has been sick the past 6 days and hasn't gone anywhere. Lisa is with him. Linda is not. I don't know if I'll ever get over being angry with him. He has changed so much recently—bad reviews on concerts, not associating with the fans, especially here in his home town. I still pray for him every day.

1975

JANUARY 1, 1975   I took our Christmas tree down and cleaned the apartment. I'm so weak and sick. I'm bored. Been working on my book. I feel guilty about not witnessing to Elvis. I'm still angry, but I love him as a Christian. I'm lonely. Want to move back to Indiana. All I can do is pray about it.

JANUARY 7, 1975   I hadn't been to the Gate for a long time. I decided to go see Fred. Only planned to stay a short while, but Harold was there, too, so I stayed until 6:00 AM! Harold drove me in the jeep up to the House. We rode all around. He took me to the barn. The horses were so starved for affection. They surrounded the jeep to prevent us from leaving. I wanted to ride one, but I was afraid Elvis would see us and we'd be in trouble. Harold raced up and down the hill with the headlights turned off. Must be a tradition around Graceland to scare all the girls by racing around the yard in the dark with all those trees! We got out of the jeep and walked to the back window of the House and peeked in. The 6'X6' TV was on. In front of it was a tall chair. We could only see the top of a person's head. The hair was dark. We figured it was Elvis. Shortly after, the man stood—it was Elvis! He walked to the stairs and went up.

Harold told me stories about him and Elvis when they were young. There was a fat girl who lived on their street. He and Elvis used to tease her endlessly. They'd stand outside her bedroom window and serenade her and run away when she appeared. They'd hide behind the outhouse and wait for her, peak in and watch her. They were so quiet, she never knew it!

Harold said Elvis NEVER made a decision on his own—he ALWAYS asked Gladys what to do. That's the problem today—he looked to his mom for everything, and now he has no one to turn to or trust. Vernon once said something mean or smart to Gladys. Elvis was furious! He threatened Vernon that, if Vernon ever spoke to Gladys like that again, he'd kill him! Also learned that this Superstar, 7th degree black belt karate expert, 40 year old man is AFRAID OF THE DARK! He has to have some kind of light on all night. He walks in his sleep. The guys take turns keeping an eye out just in case he does. They don't want him to be hurt. I don't know if I can believe all this stuff. Harold likes to brag. I enjoy listening, anyway.

JANUARY 8, 1975   Elvis' 40th birthday. Harold told me Elvis is so depressed and he hasn't left the House for over 2 weeks. He said Elvis told him a long time ago that he would not live past the age of 42—the age Gladys died. Pauline called from England She misses Elvis and Memphis.

JANUARY 10, 1975   "Jailhouse Rock" was on TV. I watched it. It's still my favorite movie! The one I fell in love with Elvis.

JANUARY 12, 1975   Got 2' of snow! Temps with wind chill are -32 degrees!

JANUARY 15, 1975   Bon's 29th birthday. I invited all the girls and the preacher's family for a surprise birthday party for her. They were all late! They finally arrived at 9:30. We all celebrated and had a good time. She was really surprised.

JANUARY 16, 1975   The phone company is going to make everyone with less than 5 years' service part time! And, they are not giving a raise to anyone this year. This sure stinks!

JANUARY 17, 1975   Went to the Gate for a while. Some silly girls had themselves packed in a crate and shipped to Elvis! The papers said the box contained puppies! The girls were scratching and whining like pups! Someone from the House said they did not order any dogs and to send them back. Vester kept kicking the crate and saying they didn't need any more dogs up at the House. The girls finally screamed and were let out of the box. They admitted they invented the scheme so they could meet Elvis! Some people sure are crazy!

JANUARY 18, 1975   Bon and the girls from church went to see a gospel group. I didn't feel well and stayed home. I'm glad I did! Lou and his friend, Billy, came to see me. I couldn't believe it! I thought he went back to his wife or died or something. He reminded me he had told me he'd be gone a month doing wrestling matches. I had forgotten. He asked me if I still want to marry him. He gave up wrestling and has a job at Krystals as a manager. I told him I will AFTER he divorces his wife. He didn't seem surprised that I knew he is still married. He said he's working on it and will hurry it up, if I will marry him! I'm so hung up on him! I do want to marry him! I'm so nervous! I told Bon. She said she will pray for us. I'm praying, too.

JANUARY 19, 1975   The story of the girls in the crate made the newspaper. Al saw them today and took them to the House. They did not see Elvis.

JANUARY 20, 1975   Went to work. They laid off 64 people from directory assistance. They say our jobs are safe for now and not to worry. Called Mom to tell her I am engaged! She's happy for me. I wish Lou would call or come so I can find out the details of the divorce and start making plans for the wedding. I'm happy and scared. I worry about if he's just using me.

JANUARY 21, 1975   Mom's birthday. Called Harold. Elvis hasn't been out of the House yet. News is 400 people from South Central Bell are laid off and 900 are now part time. Operators are not affected. Thank God! I keep praying.

JANUARY 24, 1975   Elvis still hasn't gone anywhere. I pray he's not sick. Harold took us up to the house, but Elvis wasn't downstairs. Haven't heard from Lou.

JANUARY 25, 1975   I went to see Margie and ask about Lou. She'll find out what is going on. Mom called and asked when I'm getting married. I told her I'm not sure. I have a horrible feeling about all this. Too much up in the air. I keep praying.

JANUARY 26, 1975   I saw an Olds parked in the apt complex. I thought it was Lou's. As I passed Margie's, I heard Lou's voice. I wanted to knock, but I went up the steps, praying all the way for a sign from God. I prayed that if it be His will, that Lou would come up to see me. He did come up. We sat down and talked. He says it may take 2 or 3 years before his divorce will be final. I know that it was about that long for Danny, when he filed for desertion, so it may be true. I told him Mom is coming down to meet him. He didn't seem upset or nervous about meeting her. He's just not sure when we can marry! My heart and mind go crazy when he kisses me. I just wish I knew for sure. I'll talk to Margie tomorrow.

JANUARY 27, 1975   Talked to Margie. Last night, when Lou was there, she told him how excited I am to be getting married and I'm planning a shower. He laughed and told her we can't marry—he's still married and living with his wife. He is NOT getting a divorce! He lied to me all along! I felt it down in my heart—things just didn't feel right. Well, just like with Danny, I'm glad I found out before it was too late. I'm numb, but I won't cry. Will have to let Mom know. Bon, the girls from church and I went to Boonegrove, Miss. to see the Imperials. I'd love to talk to the group about how I could reach Elvis to witness to him.

January 29, 1975   I saw Lou's car outside the apt. I sneaked out. I don't want to see him again. He's not the one for me. I'm going to go about God's work and forget about getting married.

JANUARY 30, 1975   Elvis was hospitalized with liver problems.

I remember a couple years ago Harold said Elvis had that problem, and they were worried then and are now that it may be hepatitis, what Gladys died from. I pray it isn't.

JANUARY 31, 1975   Vernon is sick. There is no one to ask how Elvis is.

FEBRUARY 1, 1975   Margie's daughter saw Lou. He asked how I was. She said she didn't know. Renee called to congratulate me on my engagement (she had talked to Mom). I told her what happened and let her know I'm OK with it. It was good to talk to her after all this time. Mom didn't seem upset when I told her about Lou. She still wants me to move back to Ind. I'm tempted. I'd see Jason every day. I want to find a guy for Bon and get her married so I can leave Memphis.

FEBRUARY 2, 1975   Elvis has a twisted colon.

FEBRUARY 5, 1975   Vernon was admitted to the hospital with chest pains.

FEBRUARY 7, 1975   Rumors are that Elvis sprained his back. No news on Vernon. They're both still hospitalized.

FEBRUARY 10, 1975   Vernon had a heart attack! Not expected to live. Leta had been here this weekend, but she didn't contact me. She figured I'd be with Lou.

FEBRUARY 11, 1975   Elvis is expected to go home in a few days.

FEBRUARY 14, 1975   Pauline called from England to see how Elvis and Vernon are doing. She said when she left last summer she felt she would never see Elvis alive again. So, she's worried.

FEBRUARY 15, 1975   Elvis is home! Vernon is improving. I watched "Girl Happy" on TV. He's not the same Elvis I know now.

FEBRUARY 21, 1975   Vernon suffered some memory loss, but

he's home. A lady from church wants me to meet a young man named Vernon. He's a Christian and single. She's going to invite him to dinner to meet me. Sounds good to me! Bon told me she's trying to get me married to Vernon and she'll move in with Sandy after Susan gets married in June! Don't know what to do! Went to a club with Carol. Nothing exciting. Wish I was dead.

     FEBRUARY 24, 1975   Leta called. She's coming down this weekend for an interview with Charlie for the fan club. She was supposed to do it on the 10th, but Charlie cancelled because Elvis was in the hospital. I discovered a lump in my breast. Have to make a doctor's appointment. I pray it's not cancer.

     FEBRUARY 25, 1975   Vernon Presley was admitted to hospital again with chest pains.

     FEBRUARY 27, 1975   Vernon Presley is home. I told Bon about the lump and the doctor's appointment. She will pray for me.

     MARCH 2, 1975   I do have a cyst. There is a new X ray machine called a mammogram. I am scheduled for the test next week. I don't need surgery at this time! Pray it will be OK.

     MARCH 5, 1975   I do not have cancer! The doctor told me what kind of cyst it is, but I was so nervous, I didn't question him any further. Unless I find another cyst, I won't need another X ray for a couple years. Thank God!

     MARCH 6, 1975   Elvis might have another concert in Memphis this year. Don't know if I'll even bother to go. Got enough nerve to call Vernon; he wasn't home.

     MARCH 7, 1975   George Klein announced Elvis will do a show in Memphis on June 10. I'm still hurt, but with all his recent illnesses, I have stopped hating him. Sandy from church had mentioned she would like to see Elvis in concert. I called and she agreed to go with me. I ordered tickets. Hope we get good seats. Mom called. She and Dad and Jason are going to KY tonight and then coming down to see me. They're going to look for a house and a job for Dad! They are moving to Memphis!   They don't want Jason to grow up in Ind.! I am so happy! I love Memphis! I love Elvis!

MARCH 16, 1975   Mom, Dad, and Jason all sang happy birthday to me on the phone. It was so sweet. While I talked to Mom, she yelled "Look at him! Look at him!" Jason took 4 steps! He's walking! On my birthday! Dad said to keep an eye open for a house for them, and if they don't find what they like, they'll build one. Great present to me!

MARCH 20, 1975   Bon's sister, Marti, flew in for a visit. Bon took vacation days to spend time with her. I'm going to Ind. for Easter.

APRIL 19, 1975   Have been so busy working and looking for houses that I didn't contact anyone from the Gate. Boy, did I miss a lot! Linda is out of Elvis' life! He bought her a home and a new car. He also bought a home and car for her parents! Elvis is dating a Play Boy bunny named Sheila Ryan. Also learned that Pris and Lisa spent Easter weekend together at Graceland with Elvis! Hope they will get back together!

APRIL 26, 1975   The Gate phone was out of order—that's why I couldn't get through when I called. Harold said Elvis was home for a few days. There was NO woman with him! He is alone! Maybe he and Pris are talking about reconciling!

MAY 4, 1975   Elvis did a benefit show in Jackson, Miss. for the tornado victims. He insisted all monies go to them. $109,000.00 was raised! Leta said Elvis had an older woman at the concert in Vegas the last time. Fred took us to the House a couple times. Leta had her interview with Charlie.

MAY 12, 1975   Mom and Dad sold their house last night! They'll be down this weekend. Got my tickets for Elvis' concert. They're on the first floor, but I don't know how far back. Tom got front row!

JUNE 10, 1975   Sandy C. and I attended Elvis' concert together. Our seats were really great. I was on the aisle, so I could move around and get pictures. I hope they turn out. Elvis was in a good mood and kept joking around with the audience. He sang pretty much the same songs. I always cry when he sings "How Great Thou Art" and the "American Triology." Sandy loved the show, too. He sang for 80 min. He introduced his dad to the audience. Linda wasn't there, and neither was Sheila, even though she's staying at the House.

JUNE 12, 1975   No one has seen Sheila leave. Linda was at the Memphian with Elvis last night, but she's not staying at the House.

JUNE 21, 1975   Mom, Dad, and Jason are here! They brought our friends Sam and Rachel. Dad and Sam have worked together for years. They want to open a construction company! Bon is staying with one of the girls from church to make room for everyone. I slept on the couch. The phone rang at 2:45 AM. It was Renee! She and David were passing through town. They called and came by to visit. What a nice surprise! We visited for a while and they went on their way.

JUNE 22, 1975   Went to church, out to lunch, and I took my family and Sam and Rachel to Graceland. Fred was on duty and had the Gates closed. When he saw me, he opened it up for me to enter. There was a large crowd there, and they were all asking "Who are they?" Dad, a big teaser, said, (pointing to me): "She's Elvis' wife, I'm his father, this (Jason) is his son." As we walked in, the crowd was gasping and yelling "That's Priscilla and Vernon!" They really believed it! Sam and Rachel were surprised that we got in. We stayed for quite a while to talk to Fred. Jason had a ball running around and looking at the horses. Fred informed me Elvis entered the hospital last night to have his eyes examined. I pray everything is OK.

JUNE 23, 1975   My family and Sam and Rachel left, but they will be back. They will move here soon!

JULY 25, 1975   Don't know what happened, but Linda is living at the House again. I wonder about Elvis—his moods change so rapidly. Sometimes he's not himself. Linda in and out! Who knows?

JULY 30, 1975   After all the hustle and bustle, Mom, Dad, Sam and Rachel are living in Memphis! They're sharing a duplex and looking for homes.

AUGUST 7, 1975   Tony decided to move to Memphis with Mom and Dad. He decided he wants to work for Elvis as a bodyguard. He went to the Gate alone. Elvis drove down, stopped and shook hands with him and several other people! It figures! I missed it again!

AUGUST 8, 1975   Bon's sister, Beth, is visiting. She and I went dancing and to the Gate for a while. Elvis came down and waved to everyone. On our way home, one of the cars from Elvis' group turned on the loudspeaker, flashed their lights, and tried to pick Beth and me up. I wasn't sure whom it was, so we just waved goodbye to them and went home.

AUGUST 15, 1975   Tony went with me to the Gate. We told Harold Tony was interested in being a guard. Harold took him to the House and had him fill out an application. Tony went to the Graceland church to look around. As he walked back to the highway toward the Gate, he saw a car parked at the entrance to the church driveway. Elvis returned with his group right behind him. The car from the church drove behind the group and went to the House! Tony ran to Harold and told him. They jumped into the jeep and flew up the driveway. Red West asked what was wrong. The guys in the strange car got out and were walking toward the House. Harold asked Red if he knew the people --he didn't. Tony, Red, Harold, and some of Elvis's Mafia started walking toward the strangers. They ran to their car and drove off. Elvis opened the House door and asked what was going on. Red told him what happened, but thanks to Tony, everything was OK. Elvis went back inside. Harold introduced Red to Tony and told him about the job application. Red told Tony, "If you want the job, you can have it. You'll start when we get back from Vegas." I can't believe it! My brother will be working for Elvis! This may be an opportunity for me to work for him, too! And, I can witness to him!

AUGUST 16, 1975   Elvis left for his Vegas tour. Guess he'll be gone a month.

AUGUST 17, 1975   April and I loved the Disney movie "Cinderella" as kids. Mr. Disney only re-released the movies every 20 years, and we wanted to see it. We stood in line with all the kids, got our tickets, bought popcorn and a drink, found a good seat and sat down. We were the only adults there. I was embarrassed. April said, "Don't worry." Some boys in the front row were acting up. April yelled at the top of her voice, "Jimmy! You sit down and behave or we're leaving!" The boys looked around, scared to death, but they sat down. No one knew April and I were the two biggest kids there enjoying every moment of the movie!

AUGUST 19, 1975   I have a strange feeling about Elvis. I keep seeing him in my mind lying in a hospital bed. I hope I'm wrong. It's the same feeling I had last time he was so sick. I'm really scared.

AUGUST 21, 1975   Elvis' tour was cancelled. He came back to Memphis and is hospitalized for exhaustion! Everyone is worried. When I tell them I envisioned it all, they just stare at me stunned. They all remember last time about my dreams!

AUGUST 26, 1975   Elvis' colon in swollen (causing his tummy to be so bloated). He also has a tooth infection and a liver disease but the doctors won't say how bad it is. I just keep praying for him.

AUGUST 27, 1975   Tony got a job. If the one for Elvis becomes available, he'll take it.

AUGUST 29, 1975   April decided to move to Hollywood and get a job at one of the movie studios as a secretary. But, she loves Memphis like I do. I feel she'll come back here to live. I'll miss her and her craziness.

SEPTEMBER 4, 1975   Got a picture of Elvis from Aileen in Ireland. The best one I've ever seen! It's a close up of his face while he's wiping it with a handkerchief. From Vegas concert last year! Gonna frame it! Dad flew to Ind. to work.

SEPTEMBER 5, 1975   Elvis left the hospital. He drove himself home at 9:15 PM. Glad he's better. Tony left for California.; he got a job there. There was an assassination attempt on President Ford. Person was captured immediately. Mom wants to see Elvis. She has been a fan since the beginning. We may go to the Gate tomorrow night. Hope she can see him!

SEPTEMBER 7, 1975   Mom, Jason, and I went to church, out to lunch, then to the Gate. I had a feeling Elvis would be down. We were there about 15 minutes when I heard engines running. I looked toward the House and saw a red mo-ped coming down. Elvis was driving it! He drove down to the Gate, stopped, smiled, and waved to Jason! Jason was excited about the bike. He kept yelling "I see a tractor!" He kept lunging forward to try to get to it—he wanted to ride it with Elvis! Mom took a picture. Hope it turns out. Elvis drove up and down several times, then out to the highway. Was glad Mom got to see him   She was excited!

SEPTEMBER 11, 1975   Arlene from Chicago is visiting. She hung around Elvis in the 60's. She says Red told her they are all worried about

Elvis cuz Elvis is on hard drugs. I've noticed the mood changes, a glassy look in his eyes for over a year now. It's also being said Joe and the Mafia are running Elvis' life, as he has no control. I pray this is wrong! All I can do is pray for him. I feel so helpless.

SEPTEMBER 23, 1975   Another assassination attempt on President Ford!

SEPTEMBER 27, 1975   Linda is OUT again. Elvis is dating one of his nurses from the hospital-- a married woman!

OCTOBER 8, 1975   Paper announced Elvis will play in Vegas the first week of Dec. I'd like to go, but I can't afford it.

OCTOBER 16, 1975   Singer Charlie Rich (he lives in Memphis) is getting a divorce. Sorry to hear that. Liz Taylor and Richard Burton remarried.

OCTOBER 17, 1975   I was hospitalized to run some tests. I have colon problems. There is nothing that can be done. I just have to live with it.

NOVEMBER 18, 1975   I kept hearing a plane flying around the house. It was flying so low. Jason and I went out to look at it. I saw "TCB" on the side and new it was Elvis' plane, the LISA MARIE that he just bought. It flew over the city almost all afternoon.

NOVEMBER 19, 1975   LISA MARIE flew around this afternoon again.

NOVEMBER 20, 1975   Harold invited me to Thanksgiving dinner with him and Elvis and the family! I couldn't believe it! What a time that would be! Thoughts kept running through my mind. Yes? No? My family? Elvis? Dinner? I thanked him for the invitation, but I feel I should be with my family. I may regret it later, but that's what I feel now. Harold sounded disappointed and told me if I change my mind, I can still go! WOW!!

NOVEMBER 27, 1975   Thanksgiving Day. Worked splits. We ate dinner in the afternoon together. I loved being with the whole family. But, I kept reminding myself and them that I could have been eating with Elvis!

DECEMBER 28, 1975   Elvis went out on his motorcycle late at night. Shirley and some others followed him to Vickers gas station. They took pics.

DECEMBER 29, 1975   The Charles Franklin Hodge Fan Club is having a birthday party on Jan. 3. Elvis is expected to attend. Security has been hired and the location, time, etc. is being kept secret. It is an invitation only event. There are many people attending! I am so happy to be part of it! I love Charlie and Elvis.

DECEMBER 31, 1975   Elvis did a New Year's Eve concert in Pontiac, Mich. He broke a record for the having largest crowd ever in attendance for any performer! He split his pants during the concert!

Charlie had made arrangements with Leta to pick him up at the Memphis airport. When the LISA MARIE landed, he called. Leta and I were going to interview Charlie for the newsletter for his fan club. As we reached the airport, we spotted Elvis' car leaving. Leta decided to follow him. She said Charlie would get a ride with one of the other guys. We caught up to the car and it was a decoy! Shortly afterward, Elvis drove by! We followed him to the Gate. We saw Lisa in the car next to her daddy. They drove up to the House. A while later, a chartered bus came and drove up to the House. Charlie was in it .

This was quite a year. I had been in and out of the hospital and so had Elvis. I was engaged and split up. Dated three guys who were interested in me, but I only wanted friendship. Fell in love with Charlie Hodge and got hurt due to a friend trying to do me a favor by telling him my feelings. Elvis was gone on tour a lot, so I hardly saw him. But, when I did see him, he wouldn't allow me to have a pic with him. It hurt me so much that I now have a love/hate relationship for the man I've loved most of my life. He knows I exist and is friendly at times, rude at others. He has changed in many ways, but so have I. The best thing is my family is living in the city I love so much. I must rely on the Lord to continue to guide me. I pray to Him every day. I know He will answer me in His time.

1976

JANUARY 3, 1976   What a day! I worked splits. I went to Mom's to have her fix my hair and to get dressed for Charlie's party. On the way, I got stopped for speeding! My first ticket in 12 years of driving! I'm all shook up! I got my time mixed up and was ½ hour late for the evening shift at work. I had put in for a furlough. The supervisor saw me dressed in my long, backless gold dress and smiled. She told me to go to the party. I was so glad!

Charlie arrived at the party about 8:15. He was surprised to see all the people—over 100 of us! Elvis sent his apologies for not coming. (George Klein announced on the radio about the party—where it was being held and that Elvis would attend!) He did not want to take away the attraction from Charlie on his big day. We were disappointed. We had hoped he would come for just a few minutes, but we understood and Charlie wasn't upset about it. We kept watching the door all night, just in case Elvis did come. He didn't.

Food and drinks were served. Charlie was laughing and drinking so much. He really enjoyed himself. He got a lot of nice gifts. One was a case of Coors beer, which is illegal, but they sneaked it in. Our gift from the club was a CB radio for his boat. I stayed close to him all night. He was so busy that I didn't talk to him except to wish him a happy birthday. He kept looking at me all evening and winking. Alabama Governor Wallace had a representative come to award Charlie with a plaque making Charlie an honorary Lieutenant Governor of Alabama! Charlie was so surprised and happy. I was proud of him.

When the party was over Charlie stood by the door and personally thanked everyone for coming. When I approached him, my fondest wish came true—Charlie kissed me! My heart flipped! He didn't kiss anyone else! I don't know why I love him. He's wild with women and drinking, but I do love him! I'm so excited! Don't know if I can sleep tonight. Glad I don't work tomorrow!

JANUARY 6, 1976   Elvis went to L.A to take Lisa home. He'll be there a few days, as he's cutting a record there.

JANUARY 7, 1976   Had an ice storm. I was voted Operator of the week! The average call takes 43 seconds—mine take 39 seconds! I also was voted the nicest operator! I'm proud, of course. But, I'm bored.

JANUARY 8, 1976   This is the first time Elvis has been gone on his birthday.

January 23, 1976   Elvis came home this morning. He's getting a racquetball court built in the back yard.

JANUARY 24, 1976   I took Gina Asaro and Rachel's daughter to the Gate. Elvis didn't come down, but we saw him standing in the front door watching as a bunch of new cars were driven up the driveway. Elvis was deciding which ones he wanted to buy. Harold took Gina and I to the back of the House, but Elvis wasn't downstairs.

JANUARY 25, 1976   Elvis saw a guy from the "old crowd" at the

Gate working at the airport and invited him to Vegas with him. The guy said Elvis' condition is terminal and not expected to live much longer! I pray he is wrong and lying!

JANUARY 26, 1976   Vic is in Memphis and looking for a place to live. I showed him our place. He likes it. He applied for an apartment. If he's approved, we'll be neighbors. Little Sandy just had a baby boy.

JANUARY 31, 1976   I don't understand why I am so depressed. I'm back with my family. I'm taking care of Jason. I have a good job. What's wrong with me?

FEBRUARY 1, 1976   Elvis had a recording studio set up in Graceland and he is recording now. Lisa's birthday.

FEBRUARY 8, 1976   Elvis finished recording the album.

FEBRUARY 17, 1976   April went to the awards show in Hollywood last night and was mobbed—the people thought she was Cher Bono! She does look like her!

FEBRUARY 19, 1976   Sue called from St. Louis to tell me Elvis is doing a concert there next month and she would get a ticket for me. I told her I don't have the money and I don't really want to go. I took my Elvis pictures down from the wall. Maybe I'm growing up finally. I still love him, but it's not the same.

FEBRUARY 29, 1976   Went to the Gate. Harold took me to the House. Elvis had just gotten his hair cut. Harold told me to pick some up off the floor. I felt the shivers as I lifted his hair. Harold told me to grab a big bunch, but I thought it was selfish. I only took a few strands. I also got a cigarette butt that was mingled in the hair! He took me outside to the garbage area and gave me carpet from the racquetball court. It's red. Guess Elvis likes red!

MARCH 6, 1976　　　　Only one of my pictures of Charlie's party turned out! I'm so mad! But, Sue sent a bunch that she took. They're really great. Wish she had gotten one of us kissing, but she didn't.

MARCH 16, 1976　　　　Can't believe I'm 28 yrs old and still not married! So depressed! Bon had the girls from church get together for cake and ice cream for me. Lots of friends called me from all over the country. Pauline had everyone at the Gate sing happy birthday to me. She's going back to Eng. tomorrow. She says she'll be back this summer.

MARCH 20, 1976　　　　Heiress Patty Hearst was found guilty after an 8 week trial. She claims she was kidnapped 2 years ago by the SLA and forced to rob a bank.

MARCH 24, 1976　　　　Pat Fowler called me to tell me about the concert last night in St. Louis. People kept jumping up on the stage trying to get to Elvis! All the guys and security were standing on stage trying to keep the people off! Elvis was so scared! He stood way in the back of the stage and ready to run off! The sad part is the St. Louis police didn't even bother to help! He only sang 45 minutes and left. I don't blame him!
Glad he wasn't hurt, and I'm glad I didn't go! I can't imagine why the cops didn't step in!

Mom, Jason, and Dad are in Indiana. I was home alone when I felt the whole room shake! Electricity and phones were down. Learned we had an earthquake! Man, was I scared! Thank God, no one was hurt.

MARCH 28, 1976   The Christian Academy is closing! All the girls from church are without jobs! Bon is hinting that she want to move back to Indiana. I guess I'll move in with Mom. They want me to, anyway.

APRIL 3, 1976   Arlene from Chicago invited me to go to Elvis' concert in Omaha April 22. She has front row seats! I told her I'll go. The tickets are for free. She will drive. We'll just share the expenses for gas, room, etc. I'll just call off sick from work.

APRIL 6, 1976   Howard Hughes died. April likes Tony Orlando (Elvis is still # 1 in her life). He's doing a concert in Memphis. She bought tickets for us. I watch his show on TV. He's very good.

APRIL 13, 1976   Patty Hearst was sentenced to 25 years in jail.

APRIL 14, 1976   There was a pic of Lisa and Vernon in the newspaper. Some kids baked an Easter cake and took it to Graceland and gave it to Lisa. She's a little doll. Patty Hearst was rushed to the hospital for emergency surgery on a collapsed lung.

APRIL 21, 1976   Arlene and I left Memphis at 11:30 P.M. She took a longer scenic route to see the country. We only stopped once-- in St. Louis-- to eat. We played games like naming all the States to stay awake. So tired!

APRIL 22, 1976   Arlene made a mistake. We were supposed to meet 2 girls in Kansas City, MO, not Kansas! So, we missed them! She drove 100 miles an hour to get to Omaha. I prayed all the way that we wouldn't get stopped or have an accident. I was scared! We made it safely.

We were lucky to get a hotel room at the Hilton, right across the street from where Elvis' concert was. I was exhausted and hungry. We didn't sleep at all. We called room service and had a sandwich brought to the room while we showered and dressed.

We had 5th row seats! I got the runs just before the show started, so I didn't see him go on stage. The stage was in the center of the room set up like the 1968 TV Special. I had to look up to see Elvis, but that was Ok. The stage was so small, and he was so close! I couldn't believe it. He sang all the oldie songs. Then, a new song, "Hurt." He sang "Little Darlin'" that I had never heard him sing before. He did a little cha cha while he sang it. It was funny. I could feel my love for him again. He kept joking, but the audience was horrible! There was hardly any applause for him. No one approached the stage to get a kiss or a scarf. I was in the center of the aisle and couldn't get out. It's the first time he did not get a standing ovation for "How Great Thou Art!" Some of us stood, but not many. Arlene and I just looked at each other like we couldn't believe it. Elvis announced he was going to sing "It's Now Or Never," my favorite song of his. I screamed cuz I was so excited. When he finished, I stood up and applauded. I was the only one. He looked at me, smiled, and nodded. I saw the hurt in his face. He didn't know what was wrong with this crowd. I thought the show was great! After he sang "I Can't Help Falling In Love With You," I tried to make my way to the stage. I couldn't get through. So many people were trying to leave and going the opposite direction as I. A lot of guys were fighting in the aisles! Unbelievable! I watched to make sure Elvis got out safely. Thank God, he did! I wasn't so sure about us, but we finally made it out. Got to bed at 1:30 AM. I had been up 28 hours, so I had no problem falling asleep.

APRIL 23, 1976   Woke up at 9:30. Ate breakfast. The write up on Elvis' show was great. The writer was surprised and wondered what was wrong with the audience. Arlene's car was acting up on the way here, but she didn't tell me. Had the back tires aligned. Left Omaha at 3:30 PM. Made one stop in St. Louis to eat.

APRIL 24, 1976   Got to Memphis at 4:00AM. Arlene wanted to go to the Gate before taking me home. They had been celebrating Harold's birthday. We stayed for quite a while talking to Pat and some others.

Bon's family was at our apartment, so I had Arlene take me to Moms. Got to bed at 9:00 AM. When Jason found me, he ran into the room and woke me. I got up and played with him until noon and went to bed. I won't make a trip like that again!

APRIL 29, 1976   Sam and Rachel left Memphis! They're moving to Alabama to be by her family. She doesn't like Memphis. I'm so surprised!

MAY 6, 1976   Got my pics back from Elvis' concert. They're great!

May 9, 1976   Mom and Dad transferred their membership to our church.

MAY 10, 1976   As I lay in bed sleeping, I heard a loud noise outside. Mom came and got me. The girl across the street was backing up to go to work and ran into my car! She doesn't want to report it to her insurance. Her parents will pay cash. I felt sorry for her. She's so young.

May 14, 1976   April missed her flight from L.A. Nothing new! She still made it on time for Tony Orlando's concert. The man is great! He's friendly, too. He got a 3 min. standing ovation! Glad we went. Went by the Gate. Charlie was playing pinball at a bar across the hwy. He is so depressed. Don't know what happened.

MAY 17, 1976   Elvis is having another concert in Memphis on July 5. Tickets are not being taken by mail. They are being sold at the Colleseum. I know I can't stand in line that long. I'll see if someone can get one for me.

MAY 18, 1976   April called me from Tom's apartment. He's getting a ticket for me for July! He's such a good guy.

May 19, 1976   Our seats are 5th row! I can't wait! On the way to the Gate, Elvis drove by on his new Harley! Nice bike!

MAY 22, 1976   April was supposed to be at work, but she stayed here. Her boss fired her. She'll have to find another job when she gets back to L.A. Charlie came down to the Gate. We showed him the Fan Club T-shirts with his pic on front. He asked if we were gonna wear them. I said, "Sure—you're the one we're coming to see!" Then, I asked him to tell Elvis to stand a little to the left so we could see Charlie. He laughed! I want to give him my phone number to call, but I'm afraid. One of the guys at the Gate has front row tickets for the concert. He's holding off to see how much money he can get!

May 26, 1976   Lorraine asked me to go to Vegas with her in Aug. I can't afford it, and I want to go to Baltimore with my family. "Wild in the Country" was on TV.

MAY 27, 1976   My hours at work are getting worse. They keep changing them. Wish I could quit. All the operators with 5 years or less service had their hours cut! The ones with seniority refuse to work overtime—they told the Union and company to put us lower ones back to work—they feel sorry for us and know we need the money.

MAY 28, 1976   Harold called the House and talked to the new guard, Tommy. He came down and took us up to see the racquetball court. It is 3 stories high!

JUNE 5, 1976   One more month til the concert!

JUNE 8, 1976   Bought Elvis' new album "From Elvis Presley Blvd." It's the one he recorded at the House a few months ago.

June 10, 1976   Went to the restaurant across the street from Graceland. Charlie was there playing pinball again. He said they're playing Vegas in Dec.

JUNE 12, 1976   "That's the Way It Is" was on TV. Good show.

JUNE 20, 1976   Aunt Pauline is here from Penn. Took her to the Gate. Fred drove her up to the House. She was so excited! We went to Tupelo and then to the brewery for their tour. At the end of the tour, there is a huge room decorated like a riverboat where they offer free samples of beer and or pop. She loves Memphis!

JUNE 22, 1976   We took Aunt Pauline for a ride on the Memphis Delta Queen. She and Jason really loved it as much as I do. There is so much to do in Memphis! People don't understand until they get here how great this city is!

JUNE 23, 1976   Went to the Gate. Elvis hasn't been out of the House since he's been home. Saw Charlie. He went to Calif. with Lisa to take her back to Pris. He is still so depressed. Wish he'd open up to me. His drinking is getting worse.

JUNE 25, 1976   Aunt Pauline went home. Mom went to the doctor. Her breasts are swollen. I pray all is OK.

JULY 4, 1976   America's Bicentennial celebration! Took Jason outside to watch the fireworks. He loved it! So excited about the concert tomorrow!

JULY 5, 1976   The concert was the greatest I'd ever seen! Elvis was alert and so funny. He lost some weight, so he looked good. Security was tight. Only a few got to the stage. The only girl he kissed was Judy from the Gate. Ramonda and Nancy got scarves. One person gave him a miniature Christmas tree. He held it up, smiled, and sang "Blue Christmas." He seldom plays the guitar, but he did tonight. Linda was there. When he introduced the band and Charlie, he stopped and looked at Charlie. "I understand you have a fan club and several of the members are here." Charlie nodded and looked to the crowd. We all stood and screamed. Elvis and Charlie laughed. Elvis asked him jokingly if he wanted to take over the rest of the show! It was so funny. He sang 1 hour and 45 minutes. I was so happy to see him at his very best, but something was upsetting me. On the way home, I was so depressed. There was an ache in my heart I couldn't explain. Someone asked what was wrong. I told her I have a feeling I'll never see Elvis again. They all said that was ridiculous.

JULY 11, 1976   Called Fred. Elvis isn't there. He either took Lisa home or went to the Elvis Convention.

JULY 12, 1976   Bon told me she's moving back to Ind. to take care of her mom. I talked it over with Mom and Dad and they told me to move in with them. I don't know where we would put all my stuff!

JULY 14, 1976   Mom had a cyst removed from her breast. It was as big as an orange! She's doing OK. No cancer! Thank God!

JULY 30, 1976   Dad put my stuff in a storage place. He has been working in Ill. and Ind. for his friend. He either drives or flies up north, depending on how long he'll be gone. It's hard to find work in construction in Memphis with a good pay. He laughed when he told me I make more money than he does here. The sad part is, it's the truth!

SEPTEMBER 7, 1976   Elvis was inducted to the MS. Hall of Fame.

SEPTEMBER 24, 1976   Mom told me the worse news in the world! They're moving back to Ind.! I can't believe it! They love it here, but the job situation for Dad is awful. They want me to go with them. I hate to give up my job. If I can get a transfer, it would be to downtown Gary, IN! I don't want to work there. It's too dangerous of an area! I'm even more depressed than I was. Don't know what to do!

SEPTEMBER 25, 1976   Took vacation time to go to Ind. with Mom and Dad to find a house. The phone company in Hammond needs me right away, so I can transfer. That's God's answer to me on what to do.

OCTOBER 2, 1976   Mom and Dad bought a house in Hobart. 3 car garage, 3 bedrooms, small kitchen, large dining area. Dad is gonna build an apartment for me in the basement. There's already a laundry area and a bath with a shower. He'll build 2 bedrooms and make a den/living room area. It will be nice, but I don't want to leave Memphis. Going back tomorrow to pack our stuff.

OCTOBER 8, 1976   My transfer from work to Hammond did not go through. The job is only part time for 3 months. I would be transferred to Indianapolis, Ind. I told them I can't take it. I'll take a leave of absence and look for another job.

OCTOBER 30, 1976   My leave of absence was approved.

NOVEMBER 2, 1976   Election Day. Jimmy Carter won. I hope he can get the country working again.

NOVEMBER 5, 1976   We packed everything and headed for KY. We'll stay the night then on to Ind.

NOVEMBER 6, 1976   The people Dad bought the house from hadn't moved yet. We stayed with Aunt Jean. "King Creole" was on. Too tired to watch it.

NOVEMBER 8, 1976   Started unpacking. Freezing and sleeting. Watched TV. "Kissin' Cousins" was on. I miss Elvis and Memphis!

NOVEMBER 10, 1976   Dad started building my apartment.

NOVEMBER 21, 1976   Went to church. I'm looking for another one. I don't feel comfortable there.

NOVEMBER 23, 1976   Jerry Lee Lewis was arrested at Graceland last night. He was drunk and was threatening to kill Elvis!

DECEMBER 1, 1976   My apartment is all done. Slept upstairs, as it's so cold downstairs. Dad will install a small furnace for me. I'll get an electric blanket tomorrow.

DECEMBER 3, 1976   Got 2 feet of snow! Didn't go out.

DECEMBER 18, 1976   Called South Central Bell. I am off the payroll—even though I took a leave for next month! I won't be paid.

DECEMBER 20, 1976   Still freezing! Mayor Daly of Chicago passed away.

DECEMBER 21, 1976   Freezing! Windchill -27!

DECEMBER 31, 1976   Still freezing and the snow won't melt. Wish it would warm up so I can look for a job. I can't get over this depression. This is the first year I have NOT been unhappy to see the year end! A horrible, horrible year!

The Final Years

1977-2012

1977

JANUARY 6, 1977   Met with Renee. She showed me pictures if Rick Sauceedo, an Elvis impersonator. She'll get us tickets for his show in March.

JANUARY 8, 1977   Elvis' 42nd birthday. Wish I was there. I keep thinking about what Harold said about Elvis not wanting to live past the age of 42. Depressed.

JANUARY 10, 1977   Still cold and snowing! Has been since we moved here. I hate it! Going to the unemployment office tomorrow to file. Mom wants me to go to General Telephone to apply for a job. I don't.

JANUARY 12, 1977   Still over 5 feet of snow on the ground! Freezing! Started writing on "Superstar" again.

JANUARY 15, 1977   Called Bon to wish her a happy 30th birthday. She's not upset about being that age. I dread it next year.

JANUARY 20, 1977   Bought a magazine. Elvis has a new girlfriend, Ginger Alden. She's 20 years old! I must admit I'm shocked. I can't figure out what happened to Elvis. He has changed so much! I still keep in touch with the group from the Gate. They send me reports and pictures from his concerts. I wish things were like they once were.

Found out I have PMS, a female menstrual and hormone problem. No wonder I've been so depressed all these years! There is no cure. Have to live with it—just like all the other health problems I have. I can only pray.

JANUARY 28, 1977   Still below freezing! It's the coldest winter her in 100 years!

FEBRUARY 1, 1977   Lisa Marie's 9th birthday.

FEBRUARY 4, 1977   Watched "Love Me Tender", A train derailed in Chicago. 100 people injured. 13 deaths.

FEBRUARY 27, 1977   Telephone company is still fighting my back pay. I'm still putting in job applications everywhere.

MARCH 1, 1977   Mom, Dad, and Jason went to Kentucky.

MARCH 9, 1977   Renee and I went to Rick Sauceedo's concert. He is so much like Elvis! It's unbelievable! Tried to get to the stage to get a scarf, but couldn't. Too many girls there—just like with Elvis! We did go back stage and got an autograph. He's very nice and was excited when I told him he's as good as Elvis.

MARCH 10, 1977   Mom called from Kentucky. Mammy is sick with gallbladder problems. They did surgery, but they don't expect her to live. They can't get the poison out of her system, and her age is against her. If she dies, I won't have a grandmother at all. Tony and I went down.

MARCH 15, 1977   Mammy died at 11:15 tonight—the exact time I felt her presence and thought of our last conversation today. I have to be strong for Mom. She's so sick, and I'll need to watch over Jason.

MARCH 16, 1977   My 29th birthday. All the family is coming for Mammy's funeral. They are taking her body to her home, as she said she did not want to go to a funeral home. I've never seen so many people here. They're from all over the county. Dad got a motel room for us so we could get some rest.

MARCH 18, 1977   Mammy's funeral. I broke down finally and cried; I couldn't stop. I didn't want to—Mom needs me!

March 22, 1977   Renee called to see if I got tickets for Elvis' concert in Chicago on May 1 and 2. I didn't even know there was one. She had tried to call while we were in KY. I'm still so numb; I don't even care that I won't see him.

MARCH 31, 1977   Telephone company won't pay unemployment.

APRIL 2, 1977   Elvis is in the hospital. He cancelled the rest of his tour. They're not sure if he will be well enough to come to Chicago or not.

APRIL 8, 1977   Elvis is supposed to be leaving the hospital. Mom is really sick. Bon's mom called me. She set up an interview for me at Edward C. Minas where she works. It's a part time job, but may go to full time. With Mom being so sick, part time will be fine.

APRIL 14, 1977   I got the job as a sales clerk at Minas! Start next week.

JUNE 10, 1977   Bon's mom introduced me to a nice, single guy named Hal. We've been dating. Only problem is he drinks too much. I won't see him much longer.

JUNE 21, 1977   A guy broke into Graceland Christian Church. He wanted to pray that he will get a ticket for Elvis' concert in Memphis in Aug.! Weird!

JUNE 26, 1977   I made friends with several ladies at work. Sue and Rita are a little younger than I, but they are Elvis fans. We clicked right away.

JULY 7, 1977   Mom had breast surgery. They stripped the insides and placed silicone implants. If she didn't, she would get cancer. She has to lie flat on her back. Tony's birthday.

JULY 31, 1977   Mom's condition is worse. Her nerves are awful. She can't do anything, and she's tired of lying down all the time. But, those are the doctor's orders. I pray so hard for her. I'm working, cleaning house, and taking care of Jason. I feel I'm on the verge of a nervous breakdown! Thank God Aunt Liz is staying with us. So depressed!

AUGUST 5, 1977   I put pictures up on my bedroom walls. I can't stand the bareness. As I put Elvis' huge poster up, I kept seeing visions of newspapers stating "Elvis is Dead! "The King of Rock N Roll is Dead!" I hear Charlie calling me on the phone and telling me Elvis is gone! I shook my head to try to clear it. I straightened the picture, stepped back. A voice in my head said, "I don't know why you put that up. You'll be taking it down soon, anyway!" I'm so scared. I can't tell anyone. They will think I am crazy! I have to be sane to take care of Mom!

AUGUST 6, 1977 Heard on the news that Elvis is getting married Sept. 12 to Ginger Alden! I can't believe it. He barely knows her. Look how long he and Pris were together before they married. Then, he had a long relationship with Linda. Red and Sonny West and Dave Hebler wrote a book "Elvis—What Happened?" and it has been released. Claims Elvis is a drug addict and gives details of crazy things Elvis has been doing. I remember Arlene telling me things Red supposedly told her. I pray they're not true! I don't want to believe it. Guess I'll never really stop loving him.

AUGUST 8, 1977 I got a LATE Christmas present from April in the mail! It's a pillowcase with a pic of Elvis!

AUGUST 12, 1977 Something is telling me to call Charlie to see if everything is OK. Kept thinking if him and Elvis all day.

AUGUST 13, 1977 So depressed. Still seeing "Elvis is Dead!" in my mind. News reports say he'll do a TV special in Oct.

AUGUST 15, 1977 Still depressed and seeing the announcement in my head that Elvis is dead! When I prayed, I asked God to watch over Elvis and I cried. I begged for forgiveness cuz I failed my mission—I didn't witness to Elvis about the Lord. I let my personal feelings for Elvis and Charlie over rule those for the Lord! I prayed to God to help me forget my feelings for Elvis. I also prayed, "Please, God, send someone to help him. Please, grant him the peace he has been seeking." I can't stop feeling guilty. I can't stop crying.

AUGUST 16, 1977 Took Mom to the doctor. He can't figure why her nerves are so bad. He gave her medicine to calm her down. I took Jason to the playground. I was so dizzy.

I felt like I was floating in the air and looking down on the earth. I could feel Elvis' presence and his eyes looking down at me. I heard voices saying he was gone. I got home and turned on the TV. "We interrupt this program to announce that singer/actor Elvis Presley died this afternoon in Memphis, Tenn. at Baptist Memorial Hospital." I was numb! "Oh! My God! No!" I walked out the front door and across the lawn. Dad was cutting the grass. He asked what was wrong. I told him. He didn't believe me. I went back into the house. Mom heard the news and was trying to calm me down. I didn't know what to do! I had dreamed this for days—this was a nightmare! I wanted to wake up!

I finally went to the phone and called the Gate. Busy. House phone. Busy. Charlie's phone. Busy. Our phone rang. Sherry called to see if I heard the news. Then Renee called. Then calls from my Memphis friends. My Lord! It was true!! The man I loved for 18 years is dead! Details are still foggy. They have to perform an autopsy. Rumors are heart attack, drug overdose, or possible respiratory failure. The public will probably never know what really happened.

I've tried to reach everyone in Memphis to find out if they know anything, but all circuits to Memphis are busy. Joe Esposito was on the news. He said Elvis' body was found on the floor of his bathroom. This is the day I've always dreaded! I can't believe this! My heart is so broken! I want to go to Memphis! I know my car won't make it! Bon is in Ft. Wayne—Renee can't go until Friday cuz she has to work. Looking at the crowds at Graceland on TV, I know I'd never get near the Gate! It's NOT like it was. I can't leave Mom—even though Aunt Liz and Hazel are here with us. What can I do? I have a feeling they'll take Elvis' body back to Graceland for the funeral services. I wonder if Vernon will let fans in to see him. That's another thing—what if I get so close but can't get in? Oh, Dear God, help me!

All the TV stations are broadcasting from Graceland. They're talking to fans. Everyone is crying. TV stations will all have specials on Elvis' life tonight after the news. The report is that Elvis had a heart attack. I remember that Harold told me 2 years ago that Elvis was afraid he wouldn't live past age 42—the same age his mom died! He didn't! And it's only 4 days difference from the day Gladys died! I can't function. I'm tending to Jason and Mom, preparing food, etc., but my heart and mind are not here—they're in Memphis. I killed Elvis! I prayed him to death by asking the Lord to grant him peace! Oh, my God! My life is over! I don't want to live! Please, God, take me HOME with You!

AUGUST 17, 1977   I didn't go to Memphis. Elvis is in Graceland, as I suspected. He will be shown to the public for only 2 hours, and the burial will be tomorrow. I can't possibly make it there on time, even if I flew. The funeral service will be closed. I'm sure there will be a lot of stars there. I feel horrible! Ramonda and Sue called—they're not going to Memphis, either. Pauline called from England. Everyone is so upset.

AUGUST 18, 1977   Elvis' body was laid to rest today. They placed him in a mausoleum near his mother's grave. His crypt will be in view through a window. Charlie drove a WHITE hearse (Elvis' favorite color for cars was white). Two girls were killed as they stood around Graceland—a car swerved into the crowd! How much worse can this get? Some of the stars that attended are: Ann-Margret, John Wayne, Sammy Davis, Jr., Charlie Pride, Caroline Kennedy and Burt Reynolds. An NBC special program after the news showed his casket being carried to his resting place. I'm living a nightmare—I wish I could wake up! Bon called to see how I'm doing. I feel my life is over. The only reason I will go on is to take care of Mom. We took her to the doctor. She can move slowly and lift very light items. She can't pick Jason up and he doesn't understand.   D o n ' t know how much more I can take.

AUGUST 19, 1977   Cleaned house to get my mind off Elvis. Mom is so depressed, and that isn't helping me, either.

AUGUST 20, 1977   Mom told me today what is bothering her: she thinks she's dying. Elvis' death didn't help matters! At least now I know.

AUGUST 21, 1977   Went to church. Post Tribune had an 8 page tribute to Elvis.

AUGUST 23, 1977   Elvis left everything to Vernon and Lisa. Vernon is to continue paying salary to those who worked for him. Lisa will inherit everything when she's 25 years old.

AUGUST 26, 1977   I want to write Charlie, but I'm not sure what to say.

AUGUST 28, 1977   I keep praying for strength and that He will send a man for me to love and marry.

AUGUST 29, 1977   I sent Charlie a note in a sympathy card. Got a newsletter from his fan club today. Don't know if Leta will keep it going or not. Some guys tried to steal Elvis' body for ransom today. Thank God they were caught!

SEPTEMBER 2, 1977   Letters from my overseas friends. They're worried about me. Pauline wants us to visit Elvis' grave together, and I agree. I couldn't do it alone. We'll have to wait and see what happens.

SEPTEMBER 16, 1977   Dad got permission from the city to build a house next door. The former owners used it for a garden. We don't need one, so Dad is going to build the same house plan he built in KY. We hope Mom will be happier.

SEPTEMBER 29, 1977   Shelby County gave permission for Elvis' and Gladys' bodies to be buried at Graceland. They will be placed in the Meditation Garden. I loved that place. So peaceful. I know Elvis would have approved. My case against the telephone co. was denied, since I refused to take the job in Indianapolis! I'll have to get a full time job.

OCTOBER 2, 1977   "Elvis: That's the Way it Is" was on. It hurt, but I watched it

.OCTOBER 3, 1977   Elvis' last concert from Indianapolis was on. He looked so tired. He was bloated. His singing even sounded weak to me. He was sick. Anyone could see that. Vernon was on to thank all the fans for everything. He looks bad. I don't think he'll live much longer. He's been sick for so long, and he really misses Elvis. I feel sorry for him.

OCTOBER 4, 1977   Elvis' and Gladys' bodies were moved today. Fans will be allowed to visit during the day.

OCTOBER 20, 1977   Shelby County announced there were 10 legal drugs in Elvis' body. All were legal and prescribed by his doctor, Dr. Nick. Several of us from the Gate feared that. I hate it!

OCTOBER 31, 1977   Bought Elvis' last album. It's a recording of his last concert that was aired on Oct. 3.

NOVEMBER 5, 1977   Dad's birthday. We moved into our new house. Dad made an apartment for me in the basement for privacy.

NOVEMBER 8, 1977   Rita, Sue and I went to Hammond to see Rick Sauceedo. Went backstage and had a pic made with him. He still is really so good! Sounds so much like Elvis, and I told him so. I cried during the show.

NOVEMBER 18, 1977   Got a thank you card from Charlie. He didn't write anything special, but I know he got my letter.

NOVEMBER 20, 1977   Ann Margret hosted a 3 hour special—"Aloha From Hawaii"—about Elvis' concerts. Sue and her sister sneaked in the last 2 nights to see Rick Sauceedo. We got him a gift—she gave it to him along with a letter we wrote to him. She said she gave him a kiss that was long enough to be from her and me! She loves Rick and Elvis!

NOVEMBER 29, 1977   Pauline and April will be in Memphis the first week of Jan. I plan to go. Rick will do a tribute to Elvis on the 8th. I asked Sue and Rita if they can go. Their parents agreed to let them go! I'm excited and sad.

DECEMBER 25, 1977   Went to Bon's mom's for a while and to Aunt Jeans for dinner. Jason was sick from all the excitement, but he got better after a nap. I pray the roads and weather will be good so we can go to Memphis. This is the first Christmas without Elvis.

DECEMBER 31, 1977   This has been the worse year of my life. I pray next year will be better.

1978

JANUARY 5, 1978   Nice weather is predicted for the next week. I'm so excited about going to Memphis! I can't sleep.

JANUARY 6, 1978   Left for Memphis at 9:30 AM. We took our time. About 23 miles from Memphis, we ran into a thick, soupy fog. It was nighttime. I couldn't even see the hood of my car! I tried following the lights of a semi, but he was going too fast. Pulled over to get gas. The owner had to get flashlights out to direct me to the highway. The closer we got to Memphis, the clearer it got. Reached the Gate at 10:45 PM. Pauline was there waiting for us. We went to Tom's apartment. April was there. We talked until 2:00

AM. Went to our hotel and to bed about 3:00. It's HOT here—in the 80's. I can't believe I'm here! Memphis will always be my home!

JANUARY 7, 1978   Got up at 8:00 AM. Had breakfast at Shoneys. Went to the Gate. No large crowds, so we got in right away. I felt so weird. I kept looking around, expecting Elvis to come driving down on a golf cart or his car. So many memories flooded my mind. I listened for his laughter. There were no girls screaming. So very quiet. So many beautiful flowers all around. One huge spray spelled out ELVIS 43. Bouquets surrounded the pool, the cross that had been at Gladys' grave in the cemetery, the Meditation Garden-- the entire area was covered with flowers. Took a lot of pictures. I looked for the horses, but they weren't out. The Trophy Room was just being built when I left, but it is finished now. Standing over Elvis' grave and looking around, I still refused to believe he's gone. My body trembled. I held back the tears, but I got sick to my stomach.

Elvis was in the process of changing his middle name legally from Aron to Aaron. Vernon fulfilled Elvis' wish. It is listed as such on his gravestone. Vernon is living in Graceland. Lisa comes to visit. I looked at the House, expecting Elvis to walk out. I could feel his presence. I have to get over this. He's really gone. When we left Graceland, I felt empty and sad, but I was glad to have seen where Elvis is at rest. I pray he has finally found peace.

JANYARY 8, 1978   Elvis' birthday. The temps dropped to 37 degrees! It snowed a little. Went to church. Then, we went walking around the shops across the street from Graceland. Elvis made Memphis rich when he was alive, and he continues to do so. The entire city has something for sale! There were copies of his marriage and death certificates, copies of the August concert tickets he wasn't able to perform. It made me sick! It's like a circus! Newspapers from Aug. 16 and 17 selling for as much as $5.00 a copy! One dollar bills with Elvis' pic sells for $2.50-$5.00! A man was selling a jumpsuit he swore Elvis wore in concert in Chicago in 1972. I knew it wasn't true! It wasn't big enough to fit me, let alone Elvis! Some of Elvis' family members were selling items they said Elvis gave them as gifts! Family members and associates are writing and selling books to reveal the "real" Elvis to the world. I want the world to remember him for what he truly was: a beautiful Southern gentleman, at times a little boy in the body of a man, an egotist at times but mostly humble, rebellious but law abiding, sexual, and religious. He was rich enough to buy whatever he wanted. He was an active man, but he was confined due to his fame. A husband who loved his wife. A father who adored his daughter. He was a loving son. A man who owned the world, but he died thinking the world owned him. A man known worldwide by his first name: Elvis. Superstar…the King of Rock N Roll—a name he didn't like. He always said there is only one King and He is in Heaven. A blessing from God to the world.   God bless his soul.

Ricks concert was fabulous! We had 2nd row seats. I cried during the whole show. The songs were great. There was a moment of silence before the show started. The last song was the "American Trilogy." A huge picture of Elvis covered the back wall. Steam rose from the stage representing clouds of Heaven. Everyone stood in awe and reverence. What a wonderful and special tribute to the greatest star ever! Sue, Rita, and I went backstage to talk to Rick. We got our pictures made with him. We raved about his performance. He humbly thanked us.

JANUARY 9, 1978   Was cold when we left Memphis. Went by the Gate to say goodbye to Vester. I'm so grateful to have been in Memphis again.

JANUARY 12, 1978   Rick is having a concert here in Feb. Ordered tickets. I'm gonna ask him for an interview with him for my book.

FEBRUARY 10, 1978   April called. She flew back to LA. She sat in front of Linda Thompson. Wonder why she's going there.

MARCH 13, 1978   Got an Elvis poster from Aileen.

MAY 7, 1978   Elvis' last concert and "Elvis On Tour" were on TV.

MAY 11, 1978   "Harum Scarum" was on.

MAY 21, 1978   Rick Sauceedo's performance was great. The Imperials and Jordanaires performed with him.

AUGUST 29, 1978   Watched Ann Margret's Elvis special on TV.

DECEMBER 18, 1978   Got Elvis' last album, "Legendary Performer III."

DECEMBER 29, 1978   I had an interview at Bank of Indiana a couple weeks ago. They called today—I got the job! I'll start on Jan. 15, Bon's birthday.

1979

JANUARY 3, 1979   Tony Orlando's show was on TV. April was in the audience and was on camera nearly the entire show! Priscilla Presley was on the show, too.

JANUARY 15, 1979   Bon's birthday. Had a storm-- over 2 feet of snow! I left 2 hours early for the job. I didn't want to be late on my first day! Hardly no one was there. They asked me to work in the mailroom and sort mail. It's not my job, but no one was there but me and my supervisor. Her name is Peggy. She's very nice.

FEBRUARY 4, 1979   TV movie, "Elvis," starring Kurt Russell was on. He did a great job! I think he'll get an award. Vernon Presley is in the hospital on a pacemaker.

JUNE 22, 1979   Bon and I both had slight crushes on Ricky Nelson as kids. He had a concert a few miles away, so we went. Had front row seats! I got a kiss and Bon took a pic of it! Why couldn't it have been that easy with Elvis? Oh, well! Had a great time. He's still very talented!

JUNE 26, 1979   Vernon Presley died. I guess Priscilla will be in charge of the estate, as Lisa is too young.

SEPTEMBER 12, 1979   Elvis' Dr. Nick is on trial for prescribing all the drugs to Elvis. He denies all charges. He also prescribed pills to Jerry Lee Lewis. If he's convicted, he may be charged with murder.

1980

FEBRUARY 4, 1980   Tony Orlando performed in Merrillville. He is great—even better than when I saw him in Memphis. As he walked down the aisles, I walked to him and gave him a rose. I got a kiss!

JUNE 23, 1980   Pris Presley had a TV special about Elvis.

1981

FEBRUARY 3, 1981   Linda Thompson's story "Elvis and the Beauty Queen" was on. What a bunch of crap! She says she left Elvis! He kicked her out! In the film, she left Graceland in a Volkswagen! Hogwash! She had 4 car loads of stuff and she was in her Lincoln! Glad he didn't marry her.

MARCH 6, 1981   Tom Jones performed in Merrillville. Good show. I tried to get to the stage to give him a flower, but the guard stopped me. So mad! All the other girls got to go up!

MARCH 30, 1981   President Ronald Reagan was shot. The shooter was caught.

MARCH 31, 1981   President Reagan is OK. Thank God.

NOVEMBER 4, 1981   Dr. Nick was acquitted of all charges! Unbelievable!

1982

JUNE 7, 1982   Graceland will be open to the public for tours! Money is needed to maintain the estate! Pris is suing Col. Parker for taking excess monies from Elvis while he was alive--50%. Lisa is the only heir; she doesn't get control until she's 25, so Pris is in charge.

1984

APRIL 5, 1984   Bon has colon cancer. She has been so sick from the chemo. She loses weight and gains it back when she's able to eat. Chemo, she loses it again. I'm afraid she thinks she's going to die soon. I pray she's wrong. I hate to see her suffer so much. She's contacting the girls from the Memphis School for a reunion. It will be nice to see them again.

MAY 24, 1984   Bon and I went to Memphis. We had no problems at all. When we reached Memphis, we were lost! Everything has built up so much! New shopping centers and stores. Finally found Poplar Blvd. and the telephone company where I worked. We made our way to Susan's where we would stay. She took us to the church we all attended. The congregation is growing so much that they had to add more space! I thank God for that. Susan and David have a sweet son, Robb. She is as nice as always. She gave up teaching and loves being a housewife!

MAY 25, 1984   Bon and I went to Graceland. There wasn't a long wait. Seems strange having to pay to get into a place that used to be my "second home"! Priscilla had the House redecorated. The reds are gone and replaced with pretty blues, the color it was when she lived there. Elvis' Aunt Delta still lives there. Several rooms are closed off. No pictures allowed. No one is allowed upstairs to Elvis' room. Elvis' records, trophies, and outfits are on display. I was nervous at first, but I began to calm down. The racquetball court was open, and there was a short movie after the tour. Talked to Harold. He's still complaining about not making enough money. He and Martha have another child. He never got a divorce. He said Pris is trying to get rid of the family members still working there and hiring all young people. Saw Vester, but didn't get a chance to talk to him. Went on the tour of the city. A lot has changed, but it's still my sweet, sweet, Memphis.

All the other girls and their families arrived. We all met at the Daniels' home for dinner. Afterward, we went to the living room to talk. Mr. Daniels got out his guitar and we sang hymns. He sneaked in "Love Me Tender" and they all sang it to me. Had a wonderful time. God has blessed all the girls with great husbands and happy lives. So glad to know that.

APRIL 26, 1984   Some of the girls went to Graceland, but the crowds were too large, so they didn't get in. Bon and I went shopping at the Mall Of Memphis. It's larger than the one in Merrillville. They're renovating Beale St. Went to Mud Island (they were discussing the plans when we lived there). There's a playground and a replica of the Miss. River. The Cotton Carnival was on, so there was a lot of activity.

APRIL 27, 1984   Went to church. Felt so good to worship there again. The Daniels kept begging us to move back to Memphis. I would love to, but it wouldn't be the same. It was sad to say goodbye to them.

APRIL 28, 1984   Memorial Day. We left Memphis around 10:00. Went to Aunt Liz' house in KY. Spent the night.

APRIL 29, 1984   Back to Ind. Took Bon to her moms. Her niece, Sara, had just gotten over the chicken pox. It's a good thing Bon did leave for the few days. (Her resistance is so low, the doctor told her to avoid all illnesses--even a cold could kill her).

DECEMBER 31, 1984   Bon has been in and out of the hospital. Her spirits are good, and she says God will cure her of the cancer. She's so weak and down to about 100 lbs. She couldn't attend the Oak Ridge Boys New Year's Eve party, so she gave her ticket to her mom. April came to visit on her way back to Calif. from Boston where she had spent Christmas. It poured rain all day and night. We enjoyed the show, but we were concerned about Bon.

1985

JANUARY 1, 1985   Chicago had a snow blizzard. O'Hare closed. April had to cancel her flight. She will have to stay here until the weather clears. We went to see Bon in the hospital. It breaks my heart. I don't think she will survive this time.

JANUARY 4, 1985   April was finally able to get a flight out. Hope she didn't lose her job.

JANUARY 8, 1985   I was so depressed when I woke up. I wanted to call off work, but I didn't. I was ill and went to the restroom. Rose came to see if I was OK. She had me sit on the couch in the lounge. Mom called Rose and asked her to relay the message to me that Bonnie had just died! I lost it. I had to go home. We went to Bon's moms' later. The neighbors were there and brought food, etc. We are all heartbroken. Our minister visited Bon and had just left when the hospital called to say she passed away. The only comforting thing is she wasn't alone. A chaplain heard her cry out and went to her. She asked him to pray for her. As he did, she whispered: "Jesus." She breathed her last. She was a sister to me. I'll miss her. I called all our friends in Memphis. Truly a sad day in our lives.

1986

MARCH 25, 1986   Mom and Dad said Jason and I could go to KY and Memphis together. We left early and stayed with Aunt Liz.

MARCH 26, 1986   Got to Memphis about 2:00PM. Picked up Sandy Young and treated her to lunch at Fridays Restaurant. Jason and I went to Mud Island first then to Graceland for the whole tour. Then, the Mall of Memphis. He loved the whole thing! He kept asking why we had to move away from here. He wanted to stay longer, but we had to get back for school on Monday. I felt more at peace leaving Memphis this time. I'll always love and miss it. But, I know my family needs me.

1997

JANUARY 21, 1997   Mom's birthday. Col. Parker died. News about him is not good. He cheated Elvis out of millions of dollars! He was a con artist from the word go. No wonder Pris was suing him!

2000

AUGUST, 2000   I have been ill for some time. I have a heavy feeling in my breast. I was hospitalized. I have a hiatal hernia and need surgery.

SEPTEMBER, 2000   The Lord guided Dr. Stanish during my surgery. In addition to the hernia repair, he realized something was wrong with my left breast. He took a biopsy—I have cancer! I was afraid it would be, but I'm not surprised to hear it. I thank God and I thank the doctor for checking it. We're waiting a few weeks for me to heal and then will do a mastectomy.

OCTOBER, 2000   A liquid cyst filled my entire breast. The mammogram I had a couple months ago did not detect it. Seven lymph nodes had to be removed. Thank God, they got it all! The reason for the cancer? Premarin that I've been taking since my hysterectomy over 20 years ago! A device will be placed under the little skin I have left to stretch it. I'll have a saline implant after that. I won't have silicone --that's what nearly killed Mom. Learned I have congestive heart failure. I cannot take the traditional intravenous chemo. I'll take pills for one week each month for six months. Then, Tamaxofin (a strong anti-cancer med) for 5 years. I thank God for His healing and loving hands. He wants me around for a reason.

2001

SEPTEMBER 11, 2001   On my way to work, the radio announced that two airplanes had flown into the Twin Towers in New York City at the World Trade Center! I started praying for the safety of all involved. There was an attack in Arlington, VA and Washington, DC! All simultaneously! When I arrived at the bank, employees were all watching the news on a small TV there. Everyone was in shock! It was almost time to open the doors for business, but we didn't know what to do. We had to wait for news from the Corporate Bank in OH. We were told to open but to be careful. Things were being investigated. We would be notified as soon as possible. A couple hours later, we were told to close for the day. Since we are so close to Chicago and our steel mills, Corporate did not want to endanger our lives. All Government offices in Chicago and Ind. were closing. When I got home, we sat at the table and watched TV the rest of the day and most of the night. The whole country was in shock! It was a nightmare! No one knows how many fatalities there are. Damage is so extensive, it may take days or weeks to be sure. This is a day in history that will never be forgotten worldwide! God bless America! God, please protect us!

2005

NOVEMBER, 2005   I will have 25 years seniority next Jan. A merger with a larger bank has created job losses for several people. Different "options"are being offered to us. But, the message is plain: they want all the senior employees OUT and replaced with younger, inexperienced workers who will work part time! My job is being eliminated at this branch and they want me to "travel" to different banks where I am needed—which can be 60 miles away! I refuse to do that! I can't just quit—I need the money, as I live on my own. Mom and Dad want me to move in with them. I'm praying extra hard for God's help.

DECEMBER, 2005   A co-worker/friend in Investments has been searching for ways to help me. She found the solution. I have been vested with the bank and I am 55 years old, so I can retire! With my pension plan and IRA, I can make it! I thank God for answering me again! I am so blessed! I'll miss all my friends I've worked with for so long, but I have to leave. They had 2 going away parties for me. On my last day, I couldn't resist saying, "Take this job and shove it!"

2006

JANUARY, 2006   I've been writing religious devotions and trying to sell them. I know God wants me to use the talent He gave me. I keep applying for disability but have been refused twice. I've sent my info to a lawyer to help. If I don't win, I don't have to pay. If I do win, I only need to pay for any back payments I may be entitled for.

AUGUST, 2006   I've been working 2 part time jobs and barely making ends meet. Dad is pleading with me to move back home. Mom has alzheimers and is getting worse. I finally agreed to it. I have to sell my furniture, give some Elvis photo albums away. But, Mom needs me.

2008

NOVEMBER 5, 2008   Dad's birthday. We had to place Mom in a nursing home several months ago. Dad, Tony, Jason and I visit daily at different hours so she's only alone at night when she sleeps. I love her so much. She kept holding my hand and looked so sad when I left. I wanted to stay, but Tony told me to go on to church.

NOVEMBER 6, 2008   Mom passed away at 2:00 this morning. We all gathered at the Home until the ambulance came to transport Mom. Dad and I made all the funeral arrangements. The pain is unbearable. I don't want to live. She was my very best friend. I wish I had stayed with her longer last night. Dad and I need each other more than ever now. God will help us through this. I want to be in Heaven with her NOW.

2009

MARCH, 2009   I was accepted for disability! Dad is so good to me. I thank God for him and my newly founded income.

2010

JANUARY 8, 2010   I was rushed to the hospital ER. I couldn't breathe, even with my oxygen on! I have pneumonia. I nearly died. I'll be hospitalized for at least 2 weeks then to rehab at the Home where Mom stayed. God wants me alive. I keep praying for His guidance. He won't desert me. I'll find a way to begin writing and spread His Word!

2011

SEPTEMBER, 2011   I discovered facebook on the computer and have decided to use it as my ministry for God. The devotions I write are printed in the church bulletin, but I feel the need to reach out to lost souls. So, while sitting comfortably at home, with the click of the keyboard on my computer, I can reach out to the world for my Lord and Savior!

OCTOBER, 2011   I've thought for a long time I was the only Elvis fan left in this area—or in the world. For several years, I had heard about an Elvis Fest at a park a few minutes away from home. I assumed it was an outdoor activity and since it's always held in the cold fall weather, I never attended. I read an ad in the newspaper that it's all indoors. Several of my face book friends are ETAs (Elvis Tribute Artists) and had entered the contest or would perform in a concert. I called Sherry to see if she would like to go. She agreed, and I ordered tickets. I'm glad we went! Had a blast. Ate, played Elvis BINGO—I won 4 Elvis prizes! We were only a few rows from the stage. A huge TV was on stage so others with seats farther back could see. The guys were all great! I loved it! I hadn't been out "on the town" like forever, so I was really impressed with everything. Got home late, but it was worth it!

NOVEMBER, 2011   An Elvis birthday tribute show in Merrillille on Jan. 7 was announced . Sherry wants to go. I ordered tickets—first row seats! I can't wait! These are all established ETAs and have all won awards. It should be a lot of fun.

DECEMBER 25, 2011   Dad and I had parts in the Christmas program at church. It went beautifully. The greatest present I received was when I saw Renee at church! Her son has been attending for a long time. I recognized the last name, but I thought he was Renee's nephew! He invited her to come, and I'm glad he did! It was so good to see her again. She's gonna attend church with us, so we'll be in touch. I told her about the Elvis concert in Jan. She's going! So, there will be three of us!

2012

JANUARY 7, 2012   Sherry, Renee, and I went to Merrillville to the Elvis Birthday Celebration. We had dinner first and discussed old times. Stars were Shawn Klush, Donny Edwards, Rick Saucedo, and Cody Slaughter. The seats were so close to the stage. I only had to stand up to touch it. All the performers went right past me when they entered or exited the stage. I got handshakes and a kiss but no scarf. I cried when Shawn sang "How Great Thou Art" and "American Trilogy." He sounded just like Elvis! All the performers received standing ovations. After the show, they met with fans. They gave autographs, allowed pics. I got a kiss from all of them. They were as kind to the fans as Elvis was. It's wonderful to know that Elvis has NOT been forgotten! His memory lives on!

JANUARY 8, 2012   Elvis' birthday. Been thinking of writing—actually finishing --the book I started 30 years ago—about Elvis. I'll have to pray about it.

JANUARY 9, 2012   I prayed last night for the Lord to tell me what I should do with my life. I heard a voice say, "Write a book." I know I have not been using the talent God has given me. I gave the excuse that none of my devotions were accepted. The voice said, "Write a book about Elvis." I thought, "Yeah, right! YOU are the One I should write about. Well, please give me a sign." I fell asleep.

JANUARY 10, 2012   I went to face book this morning. The first email I received said, "The way you write, you should write a book. You know a lot about Elvis. Why don't you write about him?" I was in shock!

I exclaimed, "All right, Dear Lord! I got the message!" I told Dad all that has happened. He agrees that it's a good idea, and he'll help me all he can. I got my diaries and picture albums out. I'll get started on it tomorrow.

JANUARY 30, 2012   Got an email from April. She has health problems. She's glad I'm writing my book and gave me some pointers.

FEBRUARY 4, 2012   Emailed April, as I've been thinking about her. I prayed that the Lord will solve her problems.

FEBRUARY 6, 2012   Got a phone call from an old Memphis friend. April died last night of heart failure! None of us can believe it! She died at the time I emailed her! Why do I get these premonitions? I feel as guilty as I did with Elvis. Dear Lord, what have I done? There is nothing I can do. Her family problems prevent us from doing anything for her. I've asked my church and all my face book friends to pray for me and her family. Donna Jones posted April and Elvis' pic for me on face book.

MARCH 30, 2012   I've finished the first draft of my book. So many people are praying for me. I've gotten responses from people who want to help me get it published and on the market. I honestly feel God wants this book done. I've found my purpose in this life!

APRIL 4, 2012   I will continue to edit this book. I will get it published, even if I publish it myself. So many options have been made available to me. God has opened my eyes and mind to so many new things. I am not famous, but I have many friends. I make mistakes, but God forgives me. I fall, but God picks me up. I cry and laugh. I feel sorrow and pain. I feel happiness. I am not rich monetarily, but I am rich with the love of my family and friends. The Lord has blessed me immensely and I am eternally grateful. I will close this chapter of my life and begin another one.

The Future

I have been blessed by three great men in my life:

DAD: He married Mom when I was eight years old and soon became and always will be my daddy.

ELVIS: I loved him with an earthly/human love a woman has for a man.

JESUS: Lord of lords and King of kings! A heavenly love that will last through all eternity!

At the END of this world, the King of kings—Jesus—will return. The earth will shake. Trumpets will blare. Angels will sing. He will, at His Father's command, step down from His heavenly throne. Every eye--from the living and the dead--will see Him. He will take His bride, His church, and His sheep to Heaven for all eternity! Praise Him! He is awesome! God bless each and every one of you!